ITALIANS

in the

UNITED STATES

A BIBLIOGRAPHY

LEWIS W. HINE/ITALIAN IMMIGRANTS ON FERRY, 1905/GEORGE EASTMAN HOUSE

ITALIANS
in the
UNITED STATES

A BIBLIOGRAPHY
OF REPORTS, TEXTS, CRITICAL STUDIES
AND RELATED MATERIALS

FRANCESCO CORDASCO

MONTCLAIR STATE COLLEGE

SALVATORE LaGUMINA

NASSAU COMMUNITY COLLEGE

Oriole Editions : New York

1972

COPYRIGHT © 1972 BY FRANCESCO CORDASCO

PUBLISHED BY ORIOLE EDITIONS, NEW YORK

LIBRARY OF CONGRESS CATALOG CARD NUMBER

78-180898

MANUFACTURED IN THE UNITED STATES

In Memory of

CARMELA MADORMA CORDASCO

1883 – 1962

urban pioneer in the tenements

CONTENTS

La letteratura sugli Stati Uniti offre modo di indagare come si e operato l'inserimento delle masse meridionali emigrate in forme di democrazia del tutto e stranee ad ogni loro precedente esperienza. Ma, forse per la stessa complessità delle questioni che investe, essa e la piu frammentaria, quella che si è articolata nel maggior numero di studi particolari e locali.

Grazie Dore, *La Democrazia e L'emigrazione in America* (1964).

The south Italian is illiterate, but not unintelligent. Traces of the "divine fire" of a race largely Pelasgic in south Italy, a race that has produced the greatest genius the world has ever seen, still persist and only await favorable environment to flash out and enrich our life. Said a hardheaded business man to Prof. Steiner, "These dagos are an ignorant lot." "Yes," was the reply, "but they are of the same race as Tasso, Dante, Verdi, Garibaldi, and Cavour." "Oh, come now, they aren't Tassos or Garibaldis." "No neither are you George Washington or Lincoln."

Antonio Mangano, *Sons of Italy: A Social And Religious Study Of The Italians In America* (1917; Russell & Russell, 1972).

In his early relations with the school, the Italo-American school child experiences a sense of inferiority in his dealings and contacts which evolves into shame of his parents' background, and eventually to a rejection of his family patterns in favor of Americans patterns. He develops a negative attitude toward the parental culture and, in the school and in situations removed from his immediate environment, ceases to identify himself with it. This rejection is practiced primarily in the school, since this is the child's main area of contact with the American world.

Leonard Covello, *The Social Background of the Italo-American School Child* (1944).

FOREWORD

The new and emerging concern with ethnic studies in American society is evident in the attention currently focused on the Italian experience in America. In a popular vein, the new affirmation of ethnicity among Italian-Americans is graphically (and somewhat truculently) recorded by Nicholas Pileggi:

> No one can be certain just when the Italian-American revolution began. It could have been September 21, 1969, when Mario Puzo's *Godfather* nudged *Portnoy* off the top of the *Times'* bestseller list; or maybe June 29, 1970, when a real godfather, in the name of unity, gathered 50,000 people around him at Columbus Circle. Perhaps it was last July, in time for the 1970 ethnic vote, when Attorney General John Mitchell ordered FBI agents to stop using the words 'Mafia' and 'Cosa Nostra' in their press releases; or maybe it will not begin until June 28 and the second Columbus Circle Unity Day rally, at which police expect a crowd of at least 150,000.

> Whatever uncertainty there may be over the exact day, there is no uncertainty over the fact that sometime within the last two years New York's Italians, after 75 years of benign residence in their own neighborhoods, have become restive. In the suburbs, while conservative, vowel-voting Italians have begun to take over the political apparatus of Nassau, Suffolk and Westchester counties, their children have been reading *The Greening of America,* just like the rest of their college friends, and have brought the middle-class Italian family its first taste of pot and filial estrangement. Those heartwarming stories in the *New York Times* about Tony the elevator operator who was given an 'honorary doctor of transportation' degree upon retiring from Baruch College, are not sitting so well with the current generation as they did with the last.[1]

In a somewhat more sedate manner, *The New York Times* commented on the same phenomenon:

> The Italians of New York do not agree about who they are, what progress they have made since the great migrations of half a century ago and where they should be going. And yet this people whose identity is so difficult to define has recently been thrust very much into the public eye....
>
> But on June 29, [1970] a remarkable thing happened to the people who have been described as being more American than the Americans. About 40,000 of them, according to the police estimate, gathered at Columbus Circle and waved the Italian tricolor. Perhaps the only Italian word many of them knew was 'ciao,' but they wore red, white and green buttons calling for 'Italian power.' After melting in the melting pot for all these years, they looked like they wanted to climb out.
>
> Here was a group New York had taken for granted. But it was also a group that never really considered itself a group, for the Italians and their descendants are notoriously independent of one another. Even in the early days, when they worked for nickels and dimes and were called wops by the immigrants who had gotten there before them, their self-help societies had been weak.
>
> But here they were, reflecting the American proclivity for group defensiveness, joining blacks, Puerto Ricans, Jews, Arabs, Mexicans, Indians, welfare recipients, the aged, conservatives, women, policemen, the New Left, drug advocates, homosexuals and Yippies in protesting for their rights.[2]

The appearance within the last few years of a number of scholarly works addressed to the study of the Italian experience in America makes clear both the importance of the experience and its relationship to the total context in which American social history is to be studied: it is only an affirmation of the fact that American history necessarily comprehends as one of its integral parts the experience of Italian immigrants and their descendants; it further records the emergence of a new cadre of scholars, largely Italian-Americans, who are finding in the new investigations the well-springs of their own cultural identity, and the invigoration of the dynamic revisionism which is recasting the framework of American history.[3] The mood of this revisionism is best articulated by an Italian-American historian in a cogent examination of some of the older theses in American immigrant historiography:

> The *contadini* of the Mezzogiorno thus came to terms with life in Chicago within the framework of their traditional pattern of thought and behavior. The social character of the south Italian peasant did not undergo a sea change, and the very nature of their adjustments to American society was dictated by their "Old World traits," which were not so much ballast to be jettisoned once they set foot on American soil. These traits and customs were the very bone and sinew of the south Italian character which proved very resistant to change even under the stress of emigration. Because it overemphasizes the power of environment and underestimates the toughness of cultural heritage, Handlin's thesis does not comprehend the experience of the immigrants from southern Italy. The basic error of this thesis is that it subordinates historical complexity to the symmetrical pattern of a sociological theory. Rather than constructing ideal types of "the peasant" or "the immigrant," the historian of immigration must study the distinctive cultural character of each ethnic group and the manner in which this influenced its adjustments in the New World.[4]

As an aid to the new examinations of the Italian American experience, earlier important scholarly works (out of print and generally unobtainable) have been reprinted;[5] that only a handful of early significant studies exists is understandable: a continuing resistance in the universities to the serious study of ethnic sub-communities largely explains the neglect of the cultural and social life of the ethnic community, and Italian life in America was not spared this neglect. Where the Italian community was studied, it was subjected to the ministrations of social workers (who concentrated on the sociopathology inevitable in a matrix of deprivation and cultural conflict) or to the probing of psychologists who sought to discern and understand the dynamics of adjustment (Williams and Child are good illustrations. See footnote No. 5). The monumental work of Robert F. Foerster (footnote No. 5) largely ignored social and cultural history and, with icy objectivity, surveyed the great watershed of Italian emigration to all parts of the world. ("By his tongue and his ways, the Italian is felt to be a 'foreigner' and even employers sometimes avoid him on that account. He has a low standard of living, and that is even an unpleasant consideration to those who wish to live better. His crowding and dirt are assumed to be his own choice; in any case are unlovely and to be avoided. His children are too numerous, and perhaps his low standard of living shows nowhere so plainly as in that pressure of baby cart upon push cart which makes the Italian streets of New York picturesque. Contempt, or at best contemptuous tolerance, prompts the vernacular epithets 'Wop,' 'Guinea,' and 'Dago.' In a country where yet the distinction between white man and black is intended as a distinction in value as well as in ethnography it is no compliment to the Italian to deny him whiteness, yet that actually happens with considerable frequency." Foerster, pp. 407-408).

Beyond the handful of early scholarly studies, there is a large primary source material which deals with the life of the Italian community in America: more often than not, these primary sources are the observations of Italian immigrants; an improvised and tendentious literature which appears under a rich mosaic of imprints, it is the very substance of the recorded life of the Italian subcommunity and in this sense, invaluable to the new American ethnic historiography. For the most part, adventitious in origin, this literature (both in Italian and English) is largely unavailable and in many instances unobtainable. It is to this primary source literature that volumes such as Antonio Mangano's *Sons of Italy* belong.[6] No guide to this literature exists, and no adequate bibliographical framework, into which this primary source material may be set, has been available. I have, in the present volume, attempted to furnish both a guide and framework for the study of the Italian experience in the United States.

The bibliography is not intended to be comprehensive; perhaps, a comprehensive listing is impracticable. Within the framework in which I have structured the entries, I have gathered together a sufficiently representative literature to afford both orientation and resources for further study. The framework [Bibliographies, Serial Publications, Guides and Directories, Miscellanea; Italian Emigration to America; Italian American History and Regional Studies; The Sociology of Italian American Life; The Italian American in the Politico-Economic Context; Italian American Life: Belles-Lettres and the Arts] is sufficiently broad to allow the inclusion of most titles, although there will be some disagreement as to where some entries more appropriately belong. In the headnotes to each of the sections, I have pointed out some of the limitations that have been observed; and, although most of the entries are not annotated, I have included some annotations where additional information was of value. The bibliography derives from many sources and a full use has been made of Velikonja's earlier compilation (No. 16, *infra*); even though Velikonja's mimeographed list was awkwardely arranged, I agree with Professor Fucilla's essentially affirmative review (*Italica*, vol. 41, June 1964, pp. 213-216) and acknowledge my indebtedness to

Professor Velikonja's earlier labors. I welcome additions and corrections.[7]

More than any other individual, Leonard Covello is both the resource and inspiration out of which this bibliography emerges: it was he who clearly understood the need and furnished the model of indefatigable and continuing attention to the Italian American experience. Additionally, my special thanks go to Professor Ernest S. Falbo; Professor Rudolph J. Vecoli; Dr. Salvatore La Gumina who furnished many titles; Dr. Salvatore A. Mondello; Professor Andrew F. Rolle; and to Dr. Luciano J. Iorizzo. Silvano M. Tomasi of the Center for Migration Studies was particularly generous in sharing ideas and resources. Angela Barone Jack struggled with a particularly difficult manuscript but managed to bring it under control. A special gratitude due to her is acknowledged.

On a personal note, I wish to record the pleasure which this volume gave me: instead of the tedium which bibliographical compendia inevitably impose, these labors carried me back into the multifariously vibrant community of my youth, and it was good, indeed, to have made the journey.

Francesco Cordasco
Upper Montclair, New Jersey
September 1971

[1]Nicholas Pileggi, "The Risorgimento of Italian Power: The Red, White and Greening of New York," *New York,* vol. 4 (June 7, 1971), p. 28. See also, Mario Puzo, "The Italians, American Style," *New York Times Magazine,* August 6, 1967.

[2]"New York's Italians: A Question of Identity," *New York Times,* November 9, 1970; see also, "Newark's New Minority, The Italians, Demands Equity," *New York Times,* August 28, 1971.

[3]See, *e.g.,* Luciano J. Iorizzo and Salvatore Mondello, *The Italian Americans* (New York: Twayne, 1971); Silvano M. Tomasi and M.H. Engel, eds., *The Italian Experience in the United States* (Staten Island, New York: Center For Migration Studies, 1970); Joseph Lopreato, *Italian Americans* (New York: Random House, 1970); Andrew F. Rolle, *The Immigrant Upraised: Italian Adventurers and Colonists in an Expanding America* (Norman: University of Oklahoma Press, 1968); Humbert S. Nelli, *The Italians in Chicago: A Study in Ethnic Mobility* (New York: Oxford

University Press, 1970); Leonard Covello, *The Social Background of the Italo-American School Child: A Study of the Southern Italian Mores and Their Effect on the School Situation in Italy and America.* Edited and with An Introduction by F. Cordasco (Leiden, The Netherlands: E.J. Brill, 1967). See also, Rudolf Glanz, *Jew and Italian: Historic Group Relations and the New Immigration, 1881-1924* (New York: Ktav Publishing Co., 1971).

[4]Rudolph J. Vecoli, "Contadini in Chicago: A Critique of *The Uprooted,*" *Journal of American History,* vol. 61 (December 1964), p. 417.

[5]*E.g.,* Robert F. Foerster, *The Italian Emigration of Our Times* [1919] (New York: Russell & Russell, 1968); Phyllis H. Williams, *South Italian Folkways in Europe and America* [1938] (New York: Russell & Russell, 1969); Irvin L. Child, *Italian or American? The Second Generation in Conflict* [1943] (New York: Russell & Russell, 1970).

[6]Beyond Antonio Mangano, *Sons of Italy: A Social and Religious Study of the Italians in America* (New York: Missionary Education Movement of the United States and Canada, 1917; Russell & Russell, 1972) see, *e.g.,* Baldo Aquilano, *L'Ordine Figli d'Italia in America* (New York: Società Tip. italiana, 1925); Amy A. Bernardy, *America Vissuta* (Torino: Fratelli Bocca Editori, 1911); Alfredo Bosi, *Cinquanti' anni di vita Italiana in America* (New York: Bagnasco Press, 1921); Robert Ferrari, *Days Pleasant and Unpleasant in the Order Sons of Italy* (New York: Mandy Press, 1926); Gaspare Nicotri, *Dalla Conca d'Oro all'Golden Gate: Studi e Impressioni di Viaggio in America* (New York: Canorna Press, 1928); Gaetano Conte, *Dieci Anni in America: Impressioni e Ricordi* (Palermo: G. Spinnato, 1903); Antonio Stella, *The Effects of Urban Congestion on Italian Women and Children* (New York: William Wood, 1908).

[7]Hopefully, the bibliography will stimulate the collection and assembly of materials on the Italian American experience; more importantly, it underscores the need for a central repository and archives for the material, preferable under a university aegis with ongoing studies in the sociology of Italian life in the United States. Unfortunately, the Casa Italiana (Columbia University) has given its attention to philology, language instruction, and peninsular history; it has never been hospitable to the study of the Italian community, and the reasons for this (since the Casa Italiana came into being because of the Italian community's generosity) are difficult to comprehend.

I. BIBLIOGRAPHIES, SERIAL PUBLICATIONS, GUIDES AND DIRECTORIES, MISCELLANEA

A. *Bibliographies*
B. *Serial Publications*
C. *Guides and Directories*
D. *Miscellanea*

I. BIBLIOGRAPHIES, SERIAL PUBLICATIONS, GUIDES AND DIRECTORIES, MISCELLANEA

A.   *Bibliographies*

Beyond the titles listed, bibliographies are available in many of the general and special works. Particularly important are Robert F. Foerster, *The Italian Emigration Of Our Times* (Cambridge: Harvard University Press, 1919; reissued with an introductory note by F. Cordasco, New York: Russell & Russell, 1968); Grazia Dore, *La Democrazia italiana e l'emigrazione in America* (Brescia: Marcelliana, 1964) which includes a bibliography of 112 pp.; the *International Migration Review,* vol. I (New Series), Summer 1967, which is a special issue devoted to the Italian American experience; and Silvano M. Tomasi and Madeline H. Engel, eds. *The Italian Experience In America* (Staten Island, New York: Center For Migration Studies, 1970) which has considerable bibliography apparatus. A corpus of late 19th century and early 20th century works (*e.g.,* by Helen Campbell, Edward N. Clopper, Hutchins Hapgood, Robert Hunter, Jacob A. Riis, John Spargo, Robert A. Woods, and Carroll D. Wright) with considerable material on Italians is available in F. Cordasco, ed., *The Social History of Poverty: The Urban Experience,* 15 vols. (New York: Garrett Press, 1969-70). See also F. Cordasco, *Sources for the Study of Economic Inequality and its Social Consequences* (New York: Augustus M. Kelly, 1971); and for the demography of the American city, see David Alloway and F. Cordasco, *Minorities and the American City* (New York: David McKay, 1970).

1. BADEN, ANNE L.   *Immigration in the United States: a selected list of recent references.* Washington, D.C.: Government Printing Office, 1943.

2. FIRKINS, INA TENEYCK.   "Italians in the United States," *Bulletin of Bibliography,* v. 8 (January, 1915), pp. 129-133.

3. GREENE, AMY BLANCHE AND GOULD, F.A.   *Handbook – bibliography on foreign language groups in the United States and Canada.* Compiled for the Committee on the New Americans of the Home Missions Council and Council of Women for Home Mission, 1925.

4. GRIFFIN, APPLETON P.C.   *A list of books on immigration [with references to periodicals].* Library of Congress, Second Issue. Washington, D.C.: Government Printing Office, 1905.

5. "IMMIGRANT GROUPS IN THE UNITED STATES,"   Russell Sage Foundation, New York. *Library Bulletin,* No. 114 (August, 1932).

6. *INTERNATIONAL MIGRATION REVIEW,* vol. I, no. 3 (Summer 1967). [Issue devoted to Italian American experience.]

7. *ITALIAN BIBLIOGRAPHY.* New York: Service Bureau for Intercultural Education, 1936.

8. *ITALIAN IMMIGRATION.* New York: Service Bureau for Intercultural Education, 1938.

9. New York Public Library. [The] *ITALIAN PEOPLE IN THE UNITED STATES.* New York: the Library, 1936. 2 vols. [A collection of clippings and pamphlets.]

10. New York Public Library. Reference Department. *HISTORY OF THE AMERICAS COLLECTION. Catalog,* vol. 12. Boston: G.K. Hall & Company, 1961.

11. "A selected list of bibliographical references and records of the Italians in the United States," *ITALIAN LIBRARY OF INFORMATION* [New York]. Outlines Series. Series 1., No. 5 (August, 1958), pp. 1-19.

12. STETLER, HENRY G., ed. *Inter-group relations bibliography (including Supplement I.), A selected list of books, periodicals, and resource agencies in inter-group relations, including a special section devoted to Connecticut studies.* Hartford, Connecticut: Connecticut State Inter-racial Commission, 1948.

13. TALBOT, WINTHROP. *Americanization. Principles of Americanism. Essentials of Americanization. Technic of Race-Assimilation.* Annotated Bibliography. 2nd edition. New York: H.W. Wilson Company, 1920.

14. TRACY, STANLEY, ed. *A report on world population migration as related to the United States of America: an exploratory survey of past studies and research on world population migration, with the view of evaluation areas already covered and outlining areas which warrant development.* Washington, D.C.: George Washington University, 1956.

15. RUSHMORE, E.M., ed. *Bibliography for social workers among foreign-born residents of the United States.* YWCA: National Board. Department of work with foreign-born women, 1920.

16. VELIKONJA, JOSEPH. *Italians in the United States.* Occasional Papers, No. 1. Department of Geography, Southern Illinois University. Carbondale, Illinois: 1963. [See *Review* (corrections), Joseph G. Fucilla, *Italica* vol. 41 (June 1964), pp. 213-216.] Awkwardly arranged, but a valuable pioneer compilation and list on the Italian experience in the United States. No annotations; includes an author index. Some copies of the mimeographed list are miscollated.

B.   *Serial Publications**

17. ATLANTICA. v. 1-22 (November 1923 - April 1940). Roma: Casa editrice della *REVISTA D'ITALIA E D'AMERICA,* 1923-1928. New York: F. Cassola, 1929-1940.

18. *BULLETIN AND ITALIANA.* v. 1 (1927-   ). Published by the Italy-America Society. [Superseded by: *Italy-America Society Bulletin.*]

19. *IL CARROCCIO.* Rivista mensile di coltura, propaganda e difesa italiana in America. v. 1. (1915-   ). New York: Il Carroccio Publishing Company.

20. *LA BASILICATA NEL MONDO: RIVISTA REGIONALE ILLUSTRATA.* v. 1-4 (1925-1927). Napoli: La Basilicata nel mondo, 1926-   . [Superseded by: *Italiani nel mondo].*

21. *COLUMBUS AMERICAN-ITALIAN REVIEW.* Anno 1. Pueblo, Colorado, 1934-

22. *IL FORO* [Giornale de la colonia lucanna in America]. Vol. 1-7 (September 1923 - April 1929). New York.

23. *LA CRITICA SOCIALE.* The social critique. Italian-American independent monthly magazine. New York: 1940.

24. *LA DONNA ITALIANA: GIORNALE DI EDUCAZIONE E DI COLTURA FEMINILE.* New York: La donna italiana Company, 1937-

25. *L'EMIGRATIO ITALIANO.*   1903 - [irregular].

26. *L'ITALIA ALL'ESTERO.*   Rivista quindicinnale di emigrazione, politica estera e coloniale. Roma, 1911-

27. *ITALAMERICA.*   New York, [July-August, 1952].

28. *ITALIA COLONIALE, REVISTA.*   Roma, 1900-1904.

29. Italian Historical Society of New York. *ITALIAN AMERICAN REVIEW,* [1966].

---

*See generally, Luigi Carnovale, Il Giornalismo degli emigranti italiani nel Nord America. Chicago, 1909. Il Progresso Italo-Americano (New York, 1880-   .) is the only Italian language daily (with Sunday Supplement and special issues) with a circulation of 75,000-80,000. Representative of a large politically oriented press is the socialist organ, Il Proletario (1896-   .) A vast number of religious periodicals was published in the Italian community. This list of serials is selective, with much of the bibliographical history and periodicity yet to be worked out by scholars.

30. *ITALIAN-AMERICAN REVIEW.* New York, v. 1-2 (1921-1922).

31. *ITALIAN NEWS SERVICE. PRESS RELEASE.* (irregular). No. 1-60 (June 11, 1940 - December 10, 1941). New York: Mazzini Society, 1940-41.

32. *GLI ITALIANI E L'AMERICA.* Rassegna nord-americana. New York: Italian-American Publishing Company, 1903-1907.

33. *THE ITALIAN SCENE.* A bulletin of cultural information. Presented by the Cultural division of the Italian Embassy. v. 1 (April, 1953-   ).

34. *ITALICA.* The quarterly bulletin of the American Association of teachers of Italian. Ann Arbor, v. 1 (1924-   ).

35. *ITALY-AMERICA MONTHLY.* (1934-35). New York: Italian Publishers. [Formed by the union of the *Bulletin of the Italy-America Society* and the *Casa Italiana Bulletin;* superseded by *Italy-America Review.]*

36. *ITALY-AMERICA REVIEW.* New York, v. 1-4 (1936-1939). [Supersedes *Italy-America Monthly].*

37. *ITALY-AMERICA SOCIETY BULLETIN.* v. 1-6, no. 8 (January, 1927 - October, 1933). New York, 1927-33. [Superseded by *Italy-America Monthly].*

38. *IL LAZIO.* periodico ... per i Laziali d'America. Anno 1-10 (1930-1939). New York: A. d'Alatri (1932-   ).

39. *IL LITTORIO.* giornale di propaganda fascista. Anno 1 (Aprile 28, 1933-   ). New York: Adria Printing & Publishing Company, 1933-

40. *MAZZINI NEWS.* (ceased publication with no. 50). No. 1-50 (February 14, 1941 - January 29, 1942). New York: Mazzini Society, 1941-42.

41. *IL MONDO.* Rivista ... di problemi internazionali. v. 1 (1938-   ). [v. 4, no. 9. date title: *Il Mondo Mensile*]. New York: Il Mondo Publishing Company.

42. *LA PAROLA.* (weekly). v. 1 (February 4, 1939-   ). New York: Published by Italian socialist federation of the Socialist party of the USA, 1939-   . [Supersedes *La Parola del popolo,* published in Chicago].

43. *LA PAROLA DEL POPOLO.* (monthly). v. 1 (September 1938-   ). Chicago: 1937-38. (Superseded by *La parola del popolo* [New York], later *La Parola.*)

44. *LA VEDETTA.* (Formerly *Il nuovo vesillo.* Settimanale di avanguardia della comunità italiana del Bronx e del Long Island.) New York: V. Capparelli, 1935-

45. *VIGO REVIEW,* New York, v. 1-2 (April 1938 - May 1939).

46. *THE VOICE OF ITALY (LA VOCE D'ITALIA): THE ITALIAN-AMERICAN NEWSPAPER.* New York, 1935.

47. *RIVISTA ITALO-AMERICANA DI LETTERE, SCIENZE ED ARTI.* Roma, 1902.

48. *THE RUBICON. A magazine on Italian and Italian-American affairs.* [Published and edited by Luigi Criscuolo]. Vol. 1-10 (1941-1957), New York.

49. UNITED AMERICA [national weekly]. Vol. 1, July 4, 1925.

C.   Guides and Directories

50. ARENA, G. F., ed.   *Directory of Italian-Americans in commerce and professions. Guida italo-americana.* Chicago: Continental Press, 1937.

51. BIANCHI, ENRICO.   *Piccola guida dell' emigrante italiano diretto agli Stati Uniti e al Canada.* Genova: Tip. Mascarello, 1924.

52. CARR, JOHN F.   *Guide to the United States of America for the Immigrant Italian.* [Prepared for the Connecticut D.A.R.] New York: Doubleday, 1911. Published also in Italian as: *Guida degli Stati Uniti per l'immigrante italiano* [1910].

53. CLOT, ALBERTO.   *Guida e consigli per gli emigranti italiani negli Stati Uniti e nel Canada.* New York: American Waldensian Aid Society, 1913.

54. *CONSIGLI ALL'EMIGRANTE.   Vade Mecum per gli Italiani negli Stati Uniti.* Firenze: Tip. Claudiana, 1912.

55. *EMIGRATO ITALIANO IN AMERICA.   Bollettino pubblicato per cura dell' Istituto S. Carlo Borromeo per l'assistenza agli italiani emigrati in America.* Roma: 1903.

56. FRESCURA, BERNARDINO.   *Guida degli Stati dell 'America del Nord con la nuova legge sull 'emigrazione.* Genova: Tip. Montorfano, 1903.

57. ELLIS, EDWARD SYLVESTER.   *Guida per gli immigranti italiani negli Stati Uniti d'America. [A guide for immigrants to the United States.]* New Jersey Immigration Commission, 1906.

58. FLAMMA, ARIO, ed.   *Italiani di America. Enciclopedia biografica.* 2 volumes. New York: Cocce Brothers, 1936-49.

59. *GUIDA DEGLI STATI UNITI CON PARTICOLARE RIGUARDO DELL' OPERA SVOLTA VI DAGLI ITALIANI.* New York: Vigo Press, 1937.

60. *LA "GUIDA ITALIANA." THE ITALIAN GUIDE.   v. 1, no. 1 [Primavera - estate 1940].* New York: Italian-American Guide Publishing Corp., 1940.

61. *ITALIAN-AMERICAN DIRECTORY.   Guida gererale per il commercio italo-americano. General guide for the Italian-American trade.* New York: Italian-American Directory Co., 1907. [Includes: "L'immigrazione italiana negli Stati Uniti d'America," pp. 85-94 of appendix; "Italian immigration to the United States," pp. 95-103 (translation of the above); "Gli italiani e la popolazione di origine italiana negli Stati Uniti d'America," pp. 105-117.]

62. *ITALIAN-AMERICAN WHO'S WHO.* A Biographical dictionary of Italian American leaders and distinguished Italian residents of the United States. v. 1 (1938-   ). New York: The Vigo Press, 1938-

63. *ITALIAN BUSINESS DIRECTORY. General guide for the Italian-American Commerce.* New York: Published under the auspices of the Italian Chamber of Commerce of New York, 1907-1912.

64. *ITALIAN DIRECTORY.* Italian Chamber of Commerce in Chicago. Chicago, October, 1927.

65. MARZO, ROBERTO. *Guida dell' emigrante negli Stati Uniti del Nord America.* Napoli: Tip. Ferrante, 1892.

66. MOLLICA, PASQUALE AND AMADEO NICOLETTI. *Guida tascabile per l'italiano in America.* New York: The Nicoletti Press, 1917.

67. *UNIONE ITALIANA D'AMERICA.* New York, 1935.

    D.   *Miscellanea [Reports, Irregular Serials]*

68. *ALMANACCO ENCICLOPEDICO ITALO-AMERICANO, 1913-1916.* Firenze: Tip. Landi, 1913-1916.

69. Columbia University. Casa Italiana. Educational Bureau. *PAMPHLETS.* No. 1-8. New York: The Cappabianca Press, 1932-1936.

70. CONGRESSO DEGLI ITALIANI ALL' ESTERO. Roma, 1918. Comitato locale di Chicago. No. 1-7. Chicago, 1908. *[Tema.]*

71. ITALIAN AMERICAN LABOR COUNCIL. *Annual Report,* 1 (1942-   ). New York, 1943-   ).

72. ITALIAN CHAMBER OF COMMERCE. *Almanac.* 1932, 1933, 1934, 1946.

73. ITALIAN HISTORICAL SOCIETY. New York. *Pamphlets.* No. 1 (1927-   ).

74. ITALIAN HISTORICAL SOCIETY. New York. *Publications,* v. 1-5 (1927-1932).

75. ITALIAN LIBRARY OF INFORMATION. *Outline Studies.* Series 1-4 (monthly-irregular). New York, 1938-41. [Closed in July 1941 by order of the U.S. Government.]

76. ITALIAN TEACHERS ASSOCIATION. *Annual Report.* No. 1 - date (1922-). New York, 1922- . (No. 11 [1931-32] published also as: Columbia University. Casa Italiana. Education Bureau. Pamphlet No. 1).

77. ITALY-AMERICA SOCIETY. *Secretary's Annual Report.* 1920-1925.

78. *IL LIBRO ANNUALE DEL LAVORATORE ITALIANO IN AMERICA.* 1927- . Chicago: Federazione italiana del partito socialista d'America, 1927-

79. *MAZZINI SOCIETY INC.* New York n.d. [Includes founders, officers, articles of incorporation.]

80. SOCIETÀ GIUSEPPE MAZZINI ITALIANA, New York. *Resoconto annuale.* ...[Annual report.] ... New York, 1926-

81. SOCIETÀ NAZIONALE DANTE ALIGHIERI - *Atti della Società Nazionale Dante Alighieri per la diffusione della lingua e della cultura italiana fuori d'Italia.* Roma, 1893-1927.

82. SOCIETÀ SAN RAFFAELE PER GL' IMMIGRANTI ITALIANI. *Rapporto annuale* (no.) 20-22 (1911-1913). New York, 1912-1914.

83. SOCIETY FOR ITALIAN IMMIGRANTS, New York. *Annual Report.* v. 1 (1906- . [*Annual Reports,* 1909-1913, New York, 1914].

II. ITALIAN EMIGRATION TO AMERICA
   A. *General Studies and Reports*
   B. *Special Studies*
   C. *Miscellanea*

UNKNOWN PHOTOGRAPHER/MULBERRY STREET, UNDATED/LIBRARY OF CONGRESS

II.   ITALIAN EMIGRATION TO AMERICA

An overview of the immigration is in U.S. Department of Commerce, Bureau of the United States, *Historical Statistics of the United States, Colonial Times to 1957* (Washington, D.C., 1960). An invaluable source is Robert Foerster, *The Italian Emigration of Our Times* (1919). The *Annual Reports* of yearly statistics on immigration and related concerns have been published since 1892, initially by the U.S. Commissioner-General of Immigration and currently by the U.S. Department of Justice, Immigration and Naturalization Service. The *Annual Reports* note the volume of immigration and its distribution by states. Particularly helpful is Niles Carpenter, *Immigrants and Their Children, 1920* (Washington, D.C.: U.S. Department of Commerce, Bureau of the Census, Monograph VI, 1927). Bibliographical annotations of statistical studies on Italian immigration have been added to the essay by Giovanni Mazzocchi, "Movemento Migratorio con l'estero" in Instituto Centrale di Statistica, *Sviluppo della populazione italiana dal 1861 al 1961* (Annali di Statistica, 94, VIII, vol. 17. Roma, 1965), pp. 769 and 787-88. For the early period, see Commissariato Generale dell' Emigrazione, *Annuario Statistico dell' Emigrazione Italiana dal 1876 al 1925 con notizie sull' emigrazione negli anni 1869-1875* (Roma, 1926); Leone Carpi, *Delle Colonie e dell' Emigrazione d'italiani all' estero sotto l'aspetto dell' industria, commercio, agricoltura, contrattazione di importanti questioni sociali* (Milano, 1874), vol. 4; Leone Carpi, *Statistica illustrata dell' emigrazione all'estero del trienno, 1874-1876 nei suoi rapporti con problemi economico-Sociali* (Roma, 1878). For recent years, see Instituto Centrale di Statistica, *Statistica delle migrazione da e per l'estero* [reports, 1926-1937]; continued from 1950 to date with *Annuario Statistico dell'emigrazione 1950-1953* (Roma, 1955), and *Annuario di Statistiche del lavoro e dell'emigrazione* (Roma, 1955-   .)

A.   General Studies and Reports

84. BECCHERINI, FRANCESCO,   *Il fenomeno dell'emigrazione italiani negli Stati Uniti.* San Sepoloro: Tip. Boncompagni, 1906.

85. BRENNA, PAOLO G.   *Storia dell'emigrazione italiana.* Roma: Libreria Cremonese, 1928.

86. CORINALDI, LEOPOLDO.   *L'emigrazione italiana negli Stati Uniti d'America.* Roma: Bertero, 1902.

87. D'AMBROSIO, MANLIO.   *Il Mezzogiorno d'Italia e l'emigrazione negli Stati Uniti.* Roma: Athenaeum, 1924. See No. 234; No. 260; No. 375.

88.* DI PALMA DI CASTIGLIONE, G.E.   *L'immigrazione italiana negli Stati Uniti d'America dal 1820 al 30 giugno 1910.* Roma: Tip. Cartiere Centrali, 1913.

89. DORE, GRAZIA.   *La Democrazia italiana e L'emigrazione in America.* Brescia: Morcelliana, 1964. (Bibliography, pp. 389-493). A major work.

90. FIDEL,   CAMILLO.   *L'emigration   italienne   aux   Etats   Unis.* France-Amerique, 1912.

91. FLORENZANO, GIOVANNI.   *Della emigrazione italiana in America comparata alle altre emigrazioni europee. Studi e proposte.* Napoli: Tip. Giannini, 1874.

92. FOERSTER,   ROBERT   F.   *The   Italian   emigration   of   our   times.* Cambridge: Harvard University Press, 1919. Reissued with an introductory note by F. Cordasco, New York: Russell & Russell, 1968. See No. 193.

93. *ITALIA.   Ministero Degli Affari Esteri - Censimento della popolazione italiana all'estero nel 1923 eseguito a cura del Commissariato dell' Emigrazione col concorso dei RR. Consoli italiani all'estero.* (Vol. I Stati Uniti, Brasile, Costarica, Cuba, Guatemala) - Vol. II Argentina, Bolivia, Columbia, Equatore). Roma: Sandron, 1925.

94. *ITALIA.   Ministero Degli Affari Esteri. Elenco di leggi decreti e regolamenti circa l'emigrazione degli Stati d'Europa e l'immigrazione e colonizzazione in America, Asia e Oceania [fino al marzo 1907].* Roma: Unione Cooperativa Editrice, 1907.

95. ITALY.   Commissariato generale dell'emigrazione. *Emigrazione e colonie. Raccolta di rapporti dei R. R. agenti diplomatici e consolari.* 3 volumes. Roma: Tipografia dell'Unione Editrice, 1903-1909. (Volume 3, part 3 includes: "Stati Uniti," pp. 1-260. A. Ravajoli. "La colonia italiana del distretto di Columbia," pp. 159-163; Gustavo Tosti. "La colonia italiana di Boston," pp. 164-167; Giacomo Fara Forni. "Gli italiani del distretto consolare di Philadelphia," pp. 168-172; Lionello Scelsi. "Il distretto viceconsolare di Pittsburgh," pp. 173-201; Giacomo Fara Forni-Luigi Villari. "Gli italiana nel distretto di Nuova Orleans," pp. 202-221; Gerolamo Naselli. "Il distretto consolare di San Francisco [California]," pp. 222-242; Giulio Riccardi. "Le condizioni del lavoro e l'emigrazione italiana in California," pp. 223-260.)

*Name also appears as G. E. Di P. Castiglione.

96. LIVI-BACCI, MASSIMO. *L'immigrazione e l'assimilazione degli italiani negli Stati Uniti secondo le statisiche demographiche Americane* (Milano: Giuffrè, 1961). [Estimates that there were in 1950 in the U.S. no fewer than 7 million people, belonging to three generations, who had at least one Italian grandparent. Other estimates have run as high as 21 million and over.] See Giuseppe Lucrezio Monticelli, "Italian Emigration: Basic characterists and Trends," in S. M. Tomasi and M. H. Engel, eds., *The Italian Experience In The United States* (1970), pp. 3-22.

97. NAPOLITANO, GAETANO. *Italia e Stati Uniti. Correnti emigratorie e commerciali.* Roma: Tip. Grafia, 1925.

98. PISANI, PIETRO. *L'immigrazione nell' America del Nord. Note e proposte.* Roma: Roma, Ufficio della Rivista Internazionale, 1911.

99. SCALABRINI, GIOVANNI BATTISTA. *L'Emigrazione Italiana in America.* Piacenza: Tip. dell'Amico del Popolo, 1887.

100. UNITED STATES IMMIGRATION COMMISSION. *Report of the Immigration Commission.* 41 vols. Washington Government Printing Office, 1911. *Index of Reports of the Immigration Commission,* S. Doc. No. 785, 61st Congress, 3rd Session, was never published. [Abstracts, vols. 1-2; includes statistical review of immigration; emigration conditions in Europe; dictionary of races or peoples; immigrants in industries; immigrants in cities; occupations of immigrants; fecundity of immigrant women; children of immigrants in schools; immigrants as charity seekers; immigration and crime; steerage conditions; bodily form of descendants of immigrants; federal immigration legislation; state immigration and alien laws; other countries; statements and recommendations.] The restrictive quotas derive from this work.

101. VILLARI, LUIGI. *Gli Stati Uniti d'America e l'emigrazione italiana.* Milano: Fratelli Treves, 1912.

B.   *Special Studies*

102. A.I. "LA COLONIZZAZIONE ITALIANA NEGLI STATI UNITI," *L'Italia coloniale,* vol. 2 (August - September, October - November, 1904), pp. 146-149, 260-266.

103. ALQUIER, MARIE-CLAUDE. *L'emigration italienne d'après-guerre en droit international public.* [Thèse pour le doctorat en droit, Toulouse, 1957.] Centre d'Edition Universitaire. Université de Toulouse, Faculté de Droit, 1957.

104. AMADORI-VIRGILI, GIOVANNI. *Il problema politico dell'emigrazione italiana.* Roma: Tip. del Popolo Romano, 1911.

105. ATTOLICO, BERNARDO. *L'ostracismo agli analfabeti negli Stati Uniti d'America.* Roma: Tipografia Unione Editrice, 1913.

106. BARBARANI, EMILIO. *Per gli emigranti e contro l'emigrazione.* Verona: Bettinelli, 1913.

107. BAMRELA, ATTILIO. *L'industria del traffico degli emigranti in Italia.* Roma: Tip. Agostiniana, 1906.

108. BASNOTTI, A.P. "Notizie sulle condizioni della navigazione italiana nel porto di New York per l'anno 1873," *Bollettino consolare* (Maggio 1874).

109. BELLI, E. *Note sull'emigrazione in America dei contadini della provincia di Treviso.* Oderzo: Bianchi, 1888.

110. BENEDUCE, ALBERTO. *Sul movimento dei rimpatriati dalle Americhe.* Roma: Tip. Libreria Moderna, 1910.

111. BENEDUCE, ALBERTO. "Capitali sottratti all'Italia dall'emigrazione all'Estero," *Giornale degli Economisti* (1904).

112. BENEDUCE, ALBERTO. *Saggio di statistica dei rimpatriati dalle Americhe.* Roma: Cooperativa tipografica Manuzio, 1911.

113. BERTAGNIOLI. *L'emigrazione dei contadini per l'America.* Fiefenze, 1887.

114. BODIO, LUIGI. *Della emigrazione italiana.* Roma: Elzeviriana, 1877.

115. BODIO, LUIGI. "Dell'emigrazione italiana," *Nuova Antologia,* v. 186 (1 Giugno 1902), pp. 529-540.

116. BODIO, LUIGI. *Statistica della emigrazione italiana all'estero nel 1881.* Roma: Società geografica italiana, 1882.

117. BOHMERT, WILHELM. "Die slavische und italienische Einwanderung in den Vereinigten Staaten." *Arbeiterfreund,* v. 46 (1908), pp. 177-196.

118. BONACCI, GIOVANNI. *Calabria e emigrazione*. Firenze: Ricci, 1908.

119. BONACCI, GIOVANNI. *Il problema dell'emigrazione nel Nord America*. Firenze: Tip. della Rassegna Nazionale, 1908.

120. BONOMELLI, GEREMIA. *L'emigrazione*. Roma: Desclee, 1912. [1899]

121. BORGHESE, PAOLO. *L'emigration italienne*. (Thèse, Univ. de Fribourg). Firenze: Fratelli Modigliani-Rossi, 1926.

122. BORTOLUCCIA, G. *Una Rassegna dell'opuscolo di S.E. Mons. G.B. Scalabrini Vescovodi Piacenza sopra l'Emigrazione Italiano in America*. (Modena: Tip. Rossi, 1887).

123. BOSCO, AUGUSTO. "La legge e la questione dell'emigrazione in Italia," *Giornale degli Economisti*, (1900).

124. BRANCHI, GIOVANNI. "L'emigrazione italiana agli Stati Uniti." *Rapporte. Bollettino del Ministero degli Affari Esteri*, (Luglio, 1895).

125. BRENNA, PAOLO. *L'emigrazione italiana nel periodo ante bellico*. Firenze: Bemparad, 1918.

126. BRINDISI, ROCCO. "L'immigrazione italiana in alcuni stati della Nuova Inghiltèrra." *Bollettino dell'Emigrazione* (1902).

127. BRUCCOLERI, GIUSEPPE. *L'emigrazione siciliana. Caratteri ed effetti secondo le piu recenti inchieste*. Roma: Cooperative Tipografica A. Manuzio, 1911.

128. BRUNIALTI, ATTILIO, "L'esodo degli italiani e la legge sull'emigrazione," *Nuova Antologia* (Luglio, 1888).

129. BUTI, G. "Note sul servizio dei rimpatri dal Nord America," *Bollettino dell'Emigrazione* (1914).

130. BYINGYON, HOMER M. "Emigration from Italy," *U.S. Consular reports*, no. 288 (September, 1904), pp. 9-11.

131. CABIATI, ATTILIO. *Il probleme dell'emigrazione protteta in Italia*. Torino: Roux e Viarengo, 1904.

132. CABRINI, ANGELO. *Il maestro degli emigranti. Guida per conferènze e preparazione degli emigranti italiani*. Imola: Tip. Galeazzi, 1912.

133. CAMPANA, FRANCESCO. *Appunti sul tèma dell'emigrazione italiana: Cause ed effetti*. Firenze: s.e., 1879.

134. CAPRA, GIUSEPPE. *La colonizzazione negli Stati Uniti*. Firenze: Istituto Agricolo Coloniale, 1916.

135. CAPUTO, ALDO. *Inchiesta sulle condizioni del lavoro agricolo e sugli effetti dell'emigrazione nella provincia de Cosenza.* Roma: Tip. Nazionale, 1909.

136. CAPUTO, ARISTIDE. *Il tesoro dell'emigrante. Guida practica dell'italiano nell'America del Nord.* Napoli: Tip. Centrale, 1903.

137. CARERI, GIUSEPPE. *Il problema dell'emigrazione italiana e la Società per l'emigrazione e colonizzazione.* Napoli: Tipografia Ferrante, 1890.

138. CARLI, FRANCESCO. *I possidenti, i contadini e l'emigrazione.* Oderzo: Tipografia Bianchi, 1888.

139. CAROCCI, CESARE. "Emigrazione italiana." *Rassegna Nazionale,* (1900).

140. CARPI, LEONE. *Delle colonie e del'emigrazione italiana all'estero sotto l'aspetto dell'industria commercio agricoltura e contrattazioni di importanti questioni sociali.* Milano: Tipografia Editrice Lombarda, 1874.*

141. CASTIGLIONE, G.E. di P. "Italian immigration into the United States 1809-1904," *American Journal of Sociology,* v. 11 (September 1905), pp. 183-206.

142. CATTAPANI, CARLO. "Gli emigranti italiani fra gli Anglo-Sassoni," *Atti, Congresso Geografico Italiano* [Palermo, 1911], pp. 143-162.

143. CAVALLI, F., "Un decennio d'attività dell'American Committee on Italian Migration." *Civiltà,* vol. 112 (June 1961), pp. 489-497.

144. CERASE, FRANCESCO P., "A Study of Italian Migrants Returning from the U.S.A.," *International Migration Review,* Vol. I. New Series (Summer 1967), pp. 67-74. See No. 316; No. 367.

145. CESARI, CESARE. *La nostra storia coloniale e l'emigrazione.* Roma: Voghera, 1905.

146. "Character Of Italian Immigration," *New England Magazine,* n.s., 35 (1906), pp. 216-220.

147. COCCHIA, ENRICO. "Il proletario intelletuale e il problema dell'emigrazione," *Nuova Antologia,* (Maggio, 1904).

148. COLETTI, FRANCESCO. "Dell'emigrazione italiana." *In Cinquanta anni di vita italiana.* Milano: Hoepli, 1912.

*See also, Leone Carpi. *Statistica illustrata dell'emmigrazione all'Estero nel Triennio 1874-1876.* Roma: Tipografia del Popolo d'Italia, 1878.

149. COLLETTI, UMBERTO M. "Gli aspetti economico-sociali della immigrazione agli Stati Uniti," *Il Carroccio*, v. 1 (May, 1915), pp. 21-28.

150. "Condizione degli emigranti dannegiati a causa della guerra," *Bollettino dell'Emigrazione* (1921).

151. "Conferenza Generale delle Organizzazioni private per la protezione degli emigranti," *Bollettino dell'Emigrazione* (1925).

152. "Congresso (il) degli Stati Uniti e l'immigrazione," *Bollettino dell' Emigrazione* (1925).

153. "Consiglio Dell'Emigrazione. Rendiconti delle sedute," *Bollettino del'- Emigrazione,* (1902-1926).

154. CONSOLINO, FILIPPO. *L'emigrazione negli Stati Uniti. Guida.* Ragusa Inferiore: Tip. Criscione, 1915.

155. CONTENTO, ALDO. *Cio che insegna l'emigrazione italiana del 1905.* Torino: Roux & Viarengo, 1906.

156. "Contingentamento dell'emigrazione italiana per gli Stati Uniti nell'opera del Commissariato Generale per l'Emigrazione," *Bollettino dell' Emigrazione,* (1924).

157. CORBINO, EPICARMO. "L'emigrazione italiana dopo la guerra e la politica relativa," *Rivista Coloniale* (Novembre 1915).

158. CORDOVA, ANTONINO. *Gli aspetti presenti e futuri dell'emigrazione.* Torino: Lattes, 1923.

159. CORRIDORE, FRANCESCO. *Una nuova fase dell'emigrazione italiana.* Torino: G.B. Paravia, 1908.

160. CURTI, GIUSEPPE. *La chiave della fortuna ossia il manuale pratico dell'emigrante italiano in America.* Torino: Tip. Salesiana, 1908.

161. DALLA VOLTA, RICCARDO. *L'analfabetismo nell'immigrazione agli Stati Uniti.* Torino: Roux & Viarengo, 1906.

162. DALLA VOLTA, RICCARDO. *Per la tutela degli emigranti.* Firenze: Seeber, 1897.

163. DALLA VOLTA, RICCARDO. *Sulle conseguenze demografiche dell'emigrazione in Italia. Atti della R. Academia dei Georgofili di Firenze.* Ricci: 1908.

164. DORE, GRAZIA. "Some social and historical aspects of Italian Emigration to America," *Journal of Social History* (Winter 1968).

165. DAVIN (COMMANDANT). "L'emigration italienne vers les deux Ameriques," *Questions diplomatiques et coloniales,* vol. 23 (16 Juin 1907), pp. 763-775.

166. DEBIASI, AGOSTINO. "Le relazioni degli italiani verso la terra d'origine e verso quella d'emigrazione," *Il Carroccio,* v. 11 (January 1916), pp. 1-15.

167. DEBONIS-DE NOBILI, IRENE. *Relazione sull'emigrazione delle donne e fanciulli nell'America del Nord.* Roma: Tip. Forenze, 1911.

168. DEGREGORIO, UMBERTO ENRICO. *L'emigrazione italiana e la guerra.* Roma: Tip. Cartiere Centrali, 1918.

169. DE LEONE, ENRICO. "Appunti per una storia dell'emigrazione italiana," *Italiani nel mondo* (10 Gennaio 1961).

170. DELLA TORRE, RODOLFO *L'emigrazione italiana prima e dopo la guerra.* Annuario del R. Liceo Scientifico Paulucci de Calboli. Forli: Tip. Rosetti, 1929.

171. DELLA VALLE–DI MIABELLO, ALESSANDRO. "Immigrazione negli Stati Uniti. Cenni statistici tolti da documenti ufficiali," *Bollettino consolare,* (Febraio 1883).

172. DE LUCA, FERDINANDO. "Emigrazione commercio e navigazione italiana negli Stati Uniti d'America. Memorie dei cav. F. DeLuca, Console Generale d'Italia a New York." *Bollettino consolare* (Giugno 1871).

173. DE PIANTI, HUMBERT. "L'émigration italienne," *Le correspondant,* v. 213 (October 25, 1903), pp. 236-251.

174. DES PLANCHES, EDMONDO MAYOR. *Attraverso gli Stati Uniti per l'emigrazione italiana.* Torino: Unione tipografica-editrice torinese, 1913.

175. DEL VECCHIO, GIULIO SALVATORE. *Sulla emigrazione permanente italiana nei paesi stranieri avvenuta nel dodicennio 1876-1887. Saggio di statistica.* Bologna: Civelli, 1892.

176. DICKINSON, JOAN Y. "Aspects of Italian immigration to Philadelphia," *Pennsylvania Magazine of History and Biography,* vol. 40 (October 1966), pp. 445-465.

177. DI COLOBIANO, LUIGI. "Sulla emigrazione agli Stati Uniti. Rapporto del cav. L. Di Colobiano, segretario della R. Legazione a Washington," *Bollettino Consolare* (Agosto 1870).

178. *DI PALMA DI CASTIGLIONE, G.E. "Dove possono andare gli italiani immigrati negli Stati Uniti," *Bollettino dell'Emigrazione* (1909).

179. *DI PALMA DI CASTIGLIONE, G.E. "Italian immigration in the United States, 1901-1904," *American Journal of Sociology.* (September 1905).

*Name also appears as G. E. Di P. Castiglione.

180. DI SAN GIULIANO, ANTONIO. L'emigrazione italiana negli Stati Uniti," *Nuova Antologia* (Luglio 1905).

181. DI VALLELONGA, G.E. "La politica dell'emigrazione italiana dopo la guerra," *Vita italiana* (Maggio 1915).

182. DINGELSTEDT, VICTOR. "Italian emigration," *Scottish Geographical Magazine*, v. 26 (1910), pp. 337-353.

183. DORE, GRAZIA. "Alcuni aspetti dei primi studi e dibattiti sull'emigrazione transoceanica," *Rassegna di politica e di storia* (Novembre 1955).

184. DUNCAN, B.O. "Italian emigration," *U.S. Consular Reports*, v. 1 (October, 1880) pp. 127-129.

185. *EMIGRAZIONE DEGLI ITALIANI IN AMERICA: recentissime notizie regolamenti lavori salari.* Forenzuola: Tip. Pennarolo, 1907.

186. "EMIGRATION FROM ITALY," *Brandstreet's*, v. 32 (September 10, 1904), p. 591.

187. FALORSI, VITTORIO. *Problemi di emigrazione dal primo congresso degli italiani all'estero alla legge Johnson.* Bologna: N. Zanichelli, 1924.

188. FAVA, BARON. *Italian immigration.* Consular reports, v. 42 (June, 1893), pp. 248-254.

189. FAVA, SAVERIO. "I linciaggi negli Stati Uniti," *Nuova Antologia* (Febbraio 1902). See No. 1183.

190. FAVO, SAVERIO. Movimento generale della immigrazione negli Stati Uniti. *Bollettino del Ministero degli Affari Esteri* (Aprile 1888).

191. FAZIO, EMILIO. "The course of European immigration, especially Italian, to the United States, 1841-1937," *Notiziario Demografico*, v. 14 (January 1914), pp. 55-57.

192. FLORENZANO, GIOVANNI. *Della emigrazione italiana in America, Comparata alle altre emigrazioni europee. Studii e proposte.* Napoli: Giannini, 1874.

193. FOERSTER, ROBERT F. "A statistical survey of Italian emigration," *Quarterly Journal of Economics*, v. 23 (November 1908), pp. 66-103. See No. 92.

194. FOULKE, WILLIAM D. "A word on Italian immigration," *Outlook*, v. 76 (February 20, 1904), pp. 459-461. (Comments by Robert De C. Ward, "Italian immigration," *Outlook*, v. 77 (May 7, 1904), pp. 95-96.

195. GALLI, GOFFREDO. "Cenni statistici sull'emigrazione e colonizzazione nell due Americhe," *Bollettino Consolare* (Dicembre 1867).

196. GANS, HERBERT, J. "Some Comments on the History of Italian Migration and on the Nature of Historical Research," *International Migration Review,* Vol. I New Series (Summer 1967), pp. 5-9.

197. GILKEY, GEORGE R. "The United States and Italy: Migration and Repatriation," *Journal of Developing Areas* (1967), pp. 23-35.

198. GINI, C. "Census of the Italian Population for 1921," *American Statistical Association,* Vol. 17 (March 1921), pp. 648-649.

199. GINI, CORRADO. "Un'inchiesta sugli emigranti italo-americani," *Genus* (Roma), v. 12, n. 1-4 (1956), pp. 3–14.

200. GLEY, WERNER. "Die Entwicklung der italienischen Auswanderung," *Zeitschrift für Erdkunde,* v. 6 (1938), pp. 768-772.

201. GODIO, GUGLIELMO. *Nuovi Orizzonti. L'America nei suoi primi fattori: La Colonizzazione e l'emigrazione.* Firenze: Barbera, 1893.

202. GROSSI, VINCENZO. "Italian emigration to America," *Chautauquan,* v. 21 (1895), pp. 270-274.

203. GROSSI, VINCENZO. "L'emigrazione italiana in America," *Nuova Antologia,* Vol. 55, (February 1895), pp. 740-757.

204. HALL, PRESCOTT F. "Italian immigration," *North American Review,* v. 163 (August 1896), pp. 252-254.

205. HAUGHWONT, FRANK G. "Italian emigration," *U.S. Consular Reports,* v. 11 (December, 1883), pp. 364-366.

206. HUNTINGTON, HENRY G. "Italian emigration to the United States," *U.S. Consular Reports,* v. 44 (February, 1894), pp. 308-309.

207. HUNTINGTON, HENRY G. "Italian emigration to the United States," *U.S. Consular Reports,* v. 45 (July, 1894), pp. 464-467.

208. "Iniziative per una pie efficace protezione degli emigranti nello Stato di New York," *Bollettino dell'Emigrazione,* (1909).

209. "Intorno a un nuovo progretto sulla immigrazione negli Stati Uniti," *Bollettino dell'Emigrazione,* (1924).

210. ITALIA. Ministero Dell'Agricoltura Industria E Commercio. *Statistica dell'emigrazione italiana all'estero negli anni 1898 e 1890 e contronti con l'emigrazione degli altri stati d'Europa. Leggi e regolamenti di alcuni stati d'Europa e d'America e colonie d'Australia sull'emigrazione e immigrazione.* Roma: Tip. Bertero, 1900. [See generally, Grazia Dore, pp. 448-455, No. 89.]

211. ITALIA.   Ministero Degli Affari Esteri. *Istruzioni per chi emigra negli Stati Uniti.* Roma: Tip. Nazionale, 1904.

212. ITALIA.   Ministero Degli Affari Esteri. *Proibizione dello sbarco negli Stati Uniti agli stranieri analfabeti.* Relazione dell'On. Consiglio dell'emigrazione. Roma: Tip. Bertero, 1914.

213. ITALIA.   *Ministero Degli Affari Esteri. Avvertenze per chi emigra negli Stati Uniti.* Roma: Bertero, 1904.

214. "ITALIAN IMMIGRATION,"   *Manufacturer's record,* v. 46 (September 22, 1904), p. 221.

215. "ITALIAN IMMIGRATION,"   *Outlook,* v. 100 (1912). p. 883.

216. ITALY.   Commissariato dell'emigrazione. *Istruzioni a chi intende emigrare per gli Stati Uniti.* Roma: Stabilimento tip. Società Cartiere Centrali, 1913.

217. ITALY.   Commissariato dell'emigrazione. *Gli italiani negli Stati Uniti e il loro risparmi.* Roma, 1920.

218. JENKS, JEREMIAH W. AND LAUCK, JETT W.   "Italians in agriculture," pp. 83-85; "Italians in the Southern States," pp. 85-88; "Italians in New York State," pp. 88-90. *The immigration problems. A study of American immigration conditions and needs.* 6th edition revised and enlarged by Rufus S. Smith. New York: Funk & Wagnalls, 1926.

219. JADOT, LOUIS.   "L'emigration italienne," *Questions diplomatiques et coloniales,* vol. 18 (August 16, 1904), pp. 209-219.

220. LANDAR, ANGELO.   *L'educazione nel Nord America e l'emigrazione del nostro proletariato intellettuale.* Roma: Unione Cooperativa Editrice, 1907.

221. "Lavori della Commissione Federale per l'immigrazione negli Stati Uniti," *Bollettino dell'Emigrazione,* (1910).

222. *La Società Italiana Di Fronte Alle Migrazione Di Massa. Studi Emigrazione,* vol. 5 (February-June, 1968). [A major work.]

223. "Legislazione sull'emigrazione e sull'immigrazione negli Stati Uniti," *Bollettino dell'Emigrazione,* (1906).

224. *L'emigrazione Italiana Negli Anni 1924 e 1925.* Relazione sui servizi dell'emigrazione presentata dal Commissario Generale. 2 volumes. Roma: Colombo, 1926.

225. "Le Società Italiane All'estero." *Bolletino del Ministero degli Affari Esteri* (April 1898); "Le Società italiane all'estero nel 1908," *Bolletino Emig.* (1908); "Le Società italiane negli Stati Uniti dell'America del Nord," *Bolletino Emig.* (1912).

226. LEVASSEUR, E.   "L'immigrazione straniera negli Stati Uniti," *Rivista italiana di sociologia,* v. 1 (1897), pp. 332-352.

227. LIBERI, ITALO.   *L'Italia in America. Notizie per gli emigranti italiani.* Genova: Tip. Pellas, 1883.

228. LOMONACO, ALFONSO.   *Da Palermo a New Orleans.* Roma: Loescher, 1898.

229. LUCATTINI, ARRIGO LUCATTINO.   *L'emigrazione italiana con note di legislazione sociale e di geografia economica.* Tortona: Tip. Vacarri, n.d.

230. MALNATE, NATALE.   *Agenti d'emigrazione.* Firenze: Uffizio Nazionale, 1911.

231. MANTEGAZZA, VICO.   *Agli Stati Uniti.* Milano: Tip. Agnelli, 1864.

232. MARIANO, JOHN HORACE.   "The Italian emigration of our times," *Il Carroccio,* v. 12 (1920), pp. 57-60. See No. 92.

233.* MAYOR DES PLANCHES, EDMONDO.   "Gli Stati Uniti e l'emigrazione italiana," *Rivista Coloniale* (1900).

234. [MEZZOGIORNO] *Associazione per lo sviluppo dell'industria nel Mezzogiorno. Statistiche sul Mezzogiorno d'Italia, 1861-1953.* Roma, 1954.

235. MORONI, G.   "L'emigrazione italiani nell' America del Nord," *Bollettino dell'emigrazione* (1913).

236. MORVILLO, GIUSEPPE.   "L'emigrazione agli Stati Uniti. Controversie e proposte," *Rivista Coloniale* (Agosto 1912).

237. MORVILLO, GIUSEPPE.   "Gli Stati Uniti e l'immigrante," *Rivista Coloniale* (Settembre 1913).

238. "Movimento Immigratorio Negli Stati Uniti Nell'anno 1920," *Bollettino dell'Emigrazione* (1923).

239. "Movimento Legislativo Negli Stati Uniti Circa L'Emigrazione," *Bollettino dell'Emigrazione* (1910).

*Name also appears as E. M. Des Planches.

240. MONTICELLI, G. LUCREZIO, "Italian Emigration: Basic Characteristics and Trends with special Reference to The Last Twenty Years" *International Migration Review,* Vol. I, New Series (Summer 1967), pp. 10-24.

241. NICOLA, GIOVANNI BATISTA. *L'emigrazione degli analfabeti e l'anima Americana.* Roma: Tip. Unione Editrice, 1917. See No. 105; No. 249.

242. *Nuova legge sull'emigrazione commentata secondo il diritto comune da un malinconico.* Genova: Tip. Marsano, 1889.

243. "Nuova legge sull'immigrazione negli Stati Uniti d'America," *Bollettino dell'Emigrazione* (1903).

244. "Nuova legge sull'immigrazione negli Stati Uniti d'America," *Bollettino dell'Emigrazione* (1907).

245. "Nuova legge degli Stati Uniti d'America concernente l'assetto dei piroscafi per emigranti," Bollettino dell'Emigrazione, (1909).

246. "Nuova legge sull'immigrazione negli Stati Uniti," *Bollettino dell'Emigrazione* (1924).

247. OLDRINI, ALEXANDER. "Italian immigration. A statement derived from the most recent statistics (1891 and first quarter 1892)," *U.S. 52nd Congress, 2nd session. Senate Report No. 1333,* pp. 265-277.

248. "Organizzazione del servizio di assistenza legale nel Nord America. Relazione dell'On." Consiglio dell'Emigrazione, *Bollettino dell'Emigrazione* (1909).

249. "Ostracismo agli analfabeti negli Stati Uniti," *Rivista Coloniale* (Febbraio 1913).

250. OTTOLENGHI, COSTANTINO. Le migrazioni del lavoro agli Stati Uniti d'America. Roma: *Giornale degli Economisti* (1900).

251. "Our Italian Immigration," *Nation,* (April 1905).

252.* PALMA DI CASTIGLIONE, G. "L'immigrazione italiana negli Stati Uniti dell'America del Nord, dal 1820 al 30 giugno 1910," *Bolletino dell'emigrazione,* (1913).

253. PANCRAZI, A. "Condizioni di lavoro e politica immigratoria negli Stati Uniti," *Bollettino dell'Emigrazione* (1919).

*Name also appears as G. E. Di P. Castiglione.

254. PEDRAZZI, ORAZIO. *Problemi dell'emigrazione italiana negli Stati Uniti.* Firenze: Tip. Ricci, 1919.

255. "Per Gli Immigrati Italiani Negli Stati Uniti d'America," *Bollettino dell'Emigrazione* (1912).

256. PERTUSIO, MARIO. "L'opera della Commissione Federale degli Stati Uniti per L'emigrazione," *Rivista d'emigrazione* (Marzo-Aprile 1912).

257. PINCITORE, ALBERICO. *Sulla maniera di risolvere il conflitto Italo-Americano.* Palermo: Tip. de Il Giornale di Sicilia, 1891.

258. "Popolazione Italiana Negli Stati Uniti d'America," *Bollettino dell' Emigrazione,* (1905).

259. POWDERLY, T.V. "Emigrazione Italiana negli Stati Uniti," *Bollettino dell'Emigrazione* (1902).

260. PREZIOSI, GIOVANNI. *Inchiesta sul Mezzogiorno e emigrazione negli Stati Uniti.* Roma: Tipografia Unione Editrice, 1911.

261. PREZIOSI, GIOVANNI. *"La proibizione dello sbarco degli analfabeti negli Stati Uniti," Vita Italiana all'Estero* (Gennaio 1903).

262. PREZIOSI, GIOVANNI. "Riforma della legge sugli infortuni invocata negli Stati Uniti dall'Ufficio Italiano del Lavoro," *Rivista Coloniale* (Dicembre 1906).

263. PREZIOSI, GIOVANNI. "La tutela dell'emigrazione e la riforma degli Istituti di protettorato negli Stati Uniti del Nord," *Rivista Coloniale,* (Luglio-Ottobre 1908).

264. PREZIOSI, GIOVANNI. "L'immigrazione italiana negli Stati Uniti," *Rivista d'Italia,* v. 1 (1898), pp. 240-259.

265. Proposte Di Modificazione Alle Leggi Sull'Emmigrazione Negli Stati Uniti," *Bollettino dell'Emigrazione* (1902).

266. RACCA, VITTORIO. "When emigrants are boomerangs," *World Outlook,* v. 3 (October 1917), p. 14.

267. RAFFO, G.B. "Emigrazione italiana agli Stati Uniti. Rapporto," *Bollettino consolare,* (Aprile 1880).

268. RAMBAUD, JACQUES. "L'emigration italienne," *Revue de Paris,* v. 12 (June 1, 1905), pp. 601-622; (June 15, 1905), pp. 871-894.

269. *RISVEGLIO COLONIALE* [Syracuse, N.Y.], May 15, 1909. [Italian immigrants' aversion to settling in the American south.].

270. ROSSI, E. "Indagini sull'emigrazione italiana all'estero, anno 1888-1889," *Memorie della Società Geografica Italiana,* v. 4 (1890).

271. ROSSI, EGISTO. "L'emigrazione italiana agli Stati Uniti. Rapporti del ca. E. Rossi Capo, agente dell'Ufficio Ellis Island (N.Y.) per la protezione degli emigranti italiani." *Bollettino del Ministero degli Affari Esteri* (Novembre 1897; April 1898; Dicembre 1898; Marzo 1900; Ottobre 1900).

272. ROSSI, EGISTO. "L'emigrazione italiana negli Stati Uniti nell'anno 1899-1900." *Italia Coloniale* (Dicembre 1900).

273. SAN GIULIANI, ANTONIO DI. "L'emigrazione italiana negli Stati Uniti," *Nuova Antologia,* v. 202 (1 Luglio 1905), pp. 88-105.

274. SANTINI, LUIGI. "Alessandro Gavazzi e l'emigrazione politico - religiosa in Inghilterra e negli Stati Uniti nel decennio 1849-1859," *Rassegna Storica del Risorgimento,* (Aprile - September 1954).

275. SCALABRINI, GIOVANNI BATTISTA. *Dell'Assistenza alla emigrazione nazionale e degli Istituti che vi provvedono.* (Piacenza: Tip. Marchesetti e Porta, 1891).

276. SCALABRINI, GIOVANNI BATTISTA. *Il disegno di legge sull'emigrazione italiana.* (Piacenza: Tip. dell'Amico del Popolo, 1888).

277. SCALABRINI, GIOVANNI BATTISTA. "L'emigrazione degli operai italiani," *Atti e documenti del XXV Congresso Cattolico Italiano.* (Venezia, 1899).

278. SCHUYLER, EUGENE. "Italian immigration into the United States," *Political Science Quarterly,* v. 4 (September, 1889), pp. 480-495.

279. SENNER, JOSEPH H. "Immigration from Italy," *North American Review,* v. 162 (May 1896), pp. 649-656. Reply by P.F. Hall, v. 163 (August 1896), pp. 252-254.

280. SOMMA, LORENZO. *Emigrazione in America. I coloni Italiani nelle tre grandi repubbliche americane.* Roma, 1907.

281. SPERANZA, GINO. *L'assistenza degli operai italiani all'Estero* (America del Nord). *Atti del II Congresso degli Italiani all'Estero.* Roma: Tipografia Editrice Nazionale, 1911.

282. SPERANZA, GINO C.   "Our Italian immigration," *Nation,* v. 80 (1905), p. 304; also, "The Italian Emigration Department in 1904," *Charities,* v. 15 (October 21, 1905), pp. 114-116.

283. STATI UNITI D'AMERICA.   "Il rimpatrio degli emigranti. Movimento emigratorio. Cento anni di immigrazione," *Bollettino dell'Emigrazione* (1919).

284. "Statistica degli emigrati italiani negli Stati Uniti (1900-1901)." *Bollettino dell'Emigrazione* (1902).

285. "Statistica dell'emigrazione italiana (1901-1925)," *Bollettino dell' Emigrazione* (1902-1925, *passim*).

286. STELLA, ANTONIO A.   *Some aspects of Italian immigration to the United States; statistical data based chiefly upon the U.S. Census and other official publications.* New York: Putnam's Sons, 1924. Reprinted, San Francisco: R & E Research Associates, 1970.

287. TEDESCHI, MARIO.   "Stati Uniti d'America," *Le prospettive dell'emigrazione italiana.* Roma: Organizzazione Editrice Tipografica, 1946.

288. THAON DI REVEL, VITTORIO.   "Delle condizioni dell'emigrazione negli Stati Uniti nell'anno 1882," Rapporto. *Bollettino Consolare,* (1884).

289. TORTESI, ARNALDO.   *Tutti in America. La questione sociale risolta con l'emigrazione.* Osimo: Tip. Querceti, 1886.

290. VILLARI, LUIGI.   Emigrazione italiana negli Stati Uniti d'America. Roma, *Nuova Antologia,* 1909.

291. VILLARI, LUIGI.   "L'emigrazione italiana negli Stati Uniti d'America," *Nuova Antologia,* v. 143 (September 16, 1909), pp. 295-311.

292. VILLARI, LUIGI.   "L'emigrazione italiana vista dagli stranieri," *Nuova Antologia,* v. 257 (February 16, 1928), pp. 475-484.

293. VILLARI, PASQUALE.   "Le consequenze della emigrazione italiana giudicate da un cittadino americano," *Nuova Antologia,* v. 215 (September, 1907), pp. 3-8.

294. VINCI, ADOLFO.   *Della tutela legale a favore dei nostri emigranti negli Stati Uniti.* Roma: Unione Editrice, 1909.

295. VOLPE LANDI, G.B.   *Circlolare del Comitato Centrale dell'Associazione di Patronato per gli Emigranti.* Rassegna Nazionale (1893).

296. VOLPE LANDI, G.B. *L'emigrazione e le sue cause, i suoi bisogni e provvedimenti*. Piacenza: Tipografia Marchesotti e Porta, 1893.

297. VOLPE LANDI, G.B., "Il problema dell'emigrazione," *Rivista Internazionale di scienza sociali, e discipline ausiliarie*, Vol. XIII (1897). pp. 500-520.

298. WATCHORN, R. "La verità sugli emigranti negli Stati Uniti," *Bollettino dell'Emigrazione* (1909).

299. WEYL, WALTER E. "Italy's exhausting emigration," *Review of Reviews*, v. 39 (February, 1905), pp. 177-182.

300. WOODS, CHARLES M. "Italian emigration," *U.S. Consular reports*, v. 31 (September, 1889), pp. 63-64.

301. WOODS, CHARLES M. "Italian emigration," *U.S. Consular reports*, v. 35 (March, 1891), pp. 329-330.

302. YVER, G. "L'emigration italienne," *Annales de geographie*, v. 6 (1897), pp. 123-132.

303. ZANICHELLI, DOMENICO. *La questione tra l'Italia e gli Stati Uniti*. Firenze: Tip. Ricci, 1891.

C.   *Miscellanea*

304. ALBERONI, FRANCESCO and GUIDO BAGLIONI. *L'Integrazione dell' immigrato nella società industrial.* (Bologna: Il Mulino, 1965). [valuable bibliographical notes]

305. BARKER, FOLGER. "What of the Italian immigrant?" *Arena,* v. 34 (August 1905), pp. 174-176.

306. BERNARDY, AMY. "Emigrazione delle donne e dei fanciulli italiani nella North Atlantic Division, Stati Uniti d'America." *Bollettino dell'Emigrazione* (1909).

307. BODIO, LUIGI. *Protection of Italian immigrants in America.* U.S. Bureau of Education (1895), v. 2, pp. 1789-1793.

308. BODIO, LUIGI. *Della protezione degli emigranti italiani in America.* Roma: Forzani, 1895.

309. BODIO, LUIGI. "The protection of the Italian emigrants in America," *Chautauquan,* v. 23 (1896), pp. 42-64.

310. BRANDENBURG, BROUGHTON. *Imported Americans. The story of the experiences of a distinguished American and his wife studying the immigration question.* New York: Frederick A. Stokes, 1904.

311. BRENNA, PAOLO. *Patria e mondo. Carmi di emigrazione e di guerra.* Firenze: Bemporad, 1925.

312. BRENNA, PAOLO. *Miraggi d'oltre oceano. Romanzo.* Firenze: Bemporad, 1922.

313. BRENNA, PAOLO. *Storia dell'emigrazione italiana.* Roma: Libreria Mantegazza, 1928.

314. CABRINI, ANGELO. *Il partito socialista e la politica del'emigrazione. Relazione al X Congresso del Partito Socialista.* Roma: Tip. Popolare, 1908.

315. CANADA. *Department of Labor. The Royal Commission appointed to Enquire into the immigration of Italian labourers to Montreal and the alleged fraudulent practice of employment agencies. Report of commissioner and evidence.* Ottawa: Dawson, 1905.

316. CERVASE, FRANCESCO. "L'emigrazione di retorno nel processo di integrazione dell'immigrato: una prima formulazione," *Genus,* vol. 33 (1967). See No. 367.

317. CHERSI, LIVIO. *Italia e Stati Uniti.* Trieste: Tip. Alabarda, 1937.

318. CIVIC LEAGUE PUBLISHING ASSOCIATION. *Per diventare Cittadino American* [c. 1910].

319. COLLETTI, UMBERTO. "The Italian Immigrant." National Conference of Charities and Corrections, *Proceedings* (1912), pp. 249-254.

320. COMETTI, ELIZABETH. "Trends in Italian emigration," *Western Political Quarterly,* v. 11 (December 1958), pp. 820-834.

321. CONOSCENTI, E. "L'Ufficio di assistenza legale per gli immigrati italiani di New York," *Bollettino dell'Emigrazione* (1907).

322. CORRADINI, ENRICO. *La Patria Lontana.* Milano: Treves, 1910.

323. CORRADINI, ENRICO. "Dall'emigrazione al nazionalismo," *Il Carroccio* (Novembre 1916).

324. *Corrispondenza settimanale dell'Ufficio Centrale dei Segretariati laici di assistenza agli emigrati.* Società Umanitaria, Milano.

325. CORSI, EDWARD. *In The Shadow Of Liberty: The Chronicle of Ellis Island.* New York: Macmillan, 1935.

326. CORSI, EDWARD. Italian Committee for the Defense of Immigrants. *Tre Anni Di Lavoro in Defesa degli Immigrati Italiani in America.* New York: Cocco Press, 1940.

327. CORRIAS. *L'Italia e le sue collettivia all'Estero.* Genova: 1923.

328. CRISCUOLO, LUIGI. *Nordic or Latin. An open letter to the honorable A. Johnson, Chairman of the Committee of Immigration of the House of Representatives.* New York, 1925.

329. DALLA VOLTA, RICCARDO. *Imperialismo Americano.* Firenze: Ricci, 1906.

330. DAVENPORT, WILLIAM E. "Italian immigration," [a letter to the editor] *Outlook,* v. 76 (February 27, 1904), p. 527.

331. DAVENPORT, WILLIAM E. "The exodus of a Latin people," *Charities,* v. 12 (May 7, 1904), pp. 463-467.

332. DE LUCIS, ANDREA. *Abusi consolari: manchevolezze dei RR. Consoli d'America.* San Francisco, Cal.: Tip. Canessa, 1918.

333. DEL VECCHIO, PIETRO. *L'emigrazione della campagna. Considerazioni.* Mondovi: Tip. Issuglio, 1871.

334. DE MICHELIS, GIUSEPPE. "Our common interest [A message from the government of Italy to the American people]," *Independent,* v. 100 (December 27, 1919), pp. 272-273.

335. DOCUMENTS ON IMMIGRATION. Mission to Italian Government. *Report of the Commissioner General of Immigration of the result of this mission to the Italian Government. October-December, 1898.* Washington: Government Printing Office, 1898.

336. "Food supplies to Italian residents in the United States," *U.S. Monthly Consular Report,* no. 333 (1908).

337. GAROSCI, ALDO, *Storia Dei Fuorusciti.* Bari, 1953.

338. GIORGIO, R. *Emigrazione, unionismo e propaganda nel Nord America.* Salerno: Tip. Spadafora, 1927.

339. GRABO, CARL H. "Americanizing the immigrants," *The Dial,* v. 66 (May 31, 1919), pp. 539-541.

340. GRANDI, ACHILLE. *Un episodio doloroso dell'emigrazione italiana in America.* Roma: Tip. Pallotta, 1878.

341. GROSE, HOWARD BENJAMIN. *Aliens or Americans?* New York: Young People's missionary movement, 1906.

342. *GUIDA DEGLI ITALIANI IN AMERICA.* New York: Tipografia dell'Eco d'Italia, 1894.

343. HARRIS, ERNEST L. "Italian emigration in foreign steamships," *U.S. Consular Reports,* no. 292 (January, 1905), pp. 292-293.

344. "Iniziative per migliorare le condizioni di vita nelle campagne e favorire l'avviamento degli immigranti all'agricoltura negli Stati Uniti d'America," *Bollettino dell' Emigrazione,* (1909).

345. INVERNIZIO, CAROLINA. *I drammi degli emigrati.* Firenze: A. Salani, 1913.

346. "Istituzioni di Patronato per gli emigranti [Society for Italian Immigrants] in New York," *Bollettino dell' Emigrazione,* (1906).

347. "Italian emigration en route: a proposed steerage reform," *Review Of Reviews,* v. 44 (1911), pp. 348-350.

348. *ITALIAN IMMIGRATION SOCIETY. Report of the commission of immigration of the State of New York.* April 5, 1909. Albany, 1909.

349. "Italian's advice to Italian immigrants," *Review Of Reviews,* v. 56 (1917), p. 100.

350. "ITALIANS," pp. 83-85 in *Dictionary of Races and Peoples,* v. 5 of the *Report of the Immigration Commission.* (61st Congress, 3rd session, v. 9) U.S. Printing Office, 1911. See No. 100.

351. *ITALIANS IN U.S.* Report of the Proceedings of conferences on immigration held in New York, September 2nd and December 12, 1906, by the Immigration department of the National Civic Federation, 1907.

352. KELLER, FRANCES A. "Who is responsible for the immigrants?" *Outlook,* v. 106 (April 25, 1914), pp. 912-917.

353. LIVOLSI, G. *Un viaggio in America.* Palermo: Tip. del Giornale di Sicilia, 1876.

354. LOPREATO, JOSEPH. *Peasants No More* (San Francisco: Chandler, 1967). [Social change in southern Italy as a consequence of emigration.]

355. MACBRAYNE, LEWIS E. "The judgment of the steerage," *Harper's Monthly Magazine,* v. 117 (September 1908), pp. 489-499.

356. McLAUGHLIN, ALLAN J. "Italian and other Latin immigrants," *Popular Science Monthly,* v. 65 (August, 1904), pp. 341-349.

357. MANGANO, ANTONIO. "The effects of emigration upon Italy," *Charities and the Commons* (January, February, April, May, June, 1908) [on causes and effects of Italian immigration.]

358. MANGANO, ANTONIO. "Camp schools for immigrants," *The Immigrants in America Review* (June, 1915).

359. MERLION, S. "Italian immigrants and their enslavement," *Forum,* v. 15 (April, 1893), pp. 183-190.

360. MORENO, CELSO CESARE. *History of a great wrong. Italian slavery in America.* [1896].

361. MULHOLLAND, THOMAS. "Ellis Island Today," *La Voce Dell'Emigrato,* Vol. 4, (May 1927), pp. 14-16.

362. North American Civic League for Immigrants, *Advice for Immigrants with special reference to New York State,* n.d.

363. North American Civic League for Immigrants. *Advice to Immigrants, Buffalo and Vicinity,* n.d.

364. PAGNINI, PIETRO. *La tubercolosi polmonare nella provincia de Lucca in raporto all'emigrazione nel Nord America e al lavoro nelle fabbriche.* Firenze: Tip. Landi, 1910. See No. 1036; No. 1037; No. 1038.

365. PARINI, PIERTO. *Gli italiani nel mondo.* Milano: Mondadori, 1937.

366. PARISI, L., *et al.* "Le colonie italiane negli Stati Uniti," *L'Italia coloniale,* v. 2 (July, 1902), pp. 53-60; (August, 1902) pp. 184-195; (September 1902), pp. 286-304; (November 1902), pp. 500-509; (December 1902), pp. 645-656; v. 1 (February 1903), pp. 194-198; (March 1903), pp. 302-309; v. 2 (July 1903), pp. 723-731; v. 1 (January - February 1904), pp. 48-58.

367. PEROTTI, ANTONIO. *Programmazione e rientro degli emigranti.* Roma: Centro Studi Emigrazione, 1967. [a major work.] See No. 144.

368. PREZIOSI, GIOVANNI. *La 'Dante Alighieri' e L'emigrazione italiana negli Stati Uniti.* Roma: Libreria Editrice Romana, 1911.

369. PRICE, WILLARD. "What I learned by traveling from Naples to New York in the steerage," *World Outlook,* v. 3 (October 1917), pp. 3-5, 14.

370. ROSS, EDWARD ALSWORTH. "The Italians," *The old world and the new. The significance of past and present immigration to American people.* New York: Century, 1914.

371. ROSELLI, BRUNO. "Our Italian Immigrants," reprinted from Henry P. Fairchild, *Immigrant Backgrounds.* New York: John Wiley & Sons, 1927.

372. ROSSI, EGISTO. "Dall'America del Nord." *Rassegna Nazionale* (1890-1893).

373. ROSSI, EGISTO. *Gli Stati Uniti e la concorrenza Americana.* Firenze: Barbera, 1884.

374. ROSSI, ADOLFO. *La Venere American. Avventure degli emigranti nel nuovo mondo.* Roma: Tip. Fantozzi, 1889.

375. RUSSO, G. *L'emigration et ses effects dans le midi de l'Italie.* Paris: Marcel Riviere, 1912.

376. SANMINIATELLI, DONATO. *Metodi d'azione per lo sviluppo della Dante Alighieri colonie italiane d'America.* Roma: Tip. Bicchieri, 1897.

377. "Scuole per Emigranti istituite dal Commissariato Generale per l'Emigrazione," *Bollettino dell' Emigrazione* (1921).

378. SHERWOOD, HERBERT FRANCIS. "Whence they came?" *Outlook,* v. 88 (February 22, 1908), pp. 407-415.

379. *SOCIETÀ DI PATRONATO PER GLI EMIGRANTI ITALIANI.* Picacenza, Tip. Marescotti, 1896.

380. SPERANZA, GINO. "Solving the Immigration Problem," *Outlook,* LXXVI (April 16, 1904), pp. 918-933.

381. SPERANZA, GINO. "È L'emigrazione italiana una minaccia?" *Italia Coloniale* (Settembre - Ottobre 1904).

382. SPERANZA, GINO. "America arraigned: Villari's *Gli Stati Uniti d'America e l'emigrazione italiana,*" *Survey,* v. 33 (October 24, 1914), pp. 84-86.

383. STEVENSON, FREDERICK B., "Italian Colonies in the United States: A New Solution for the Immigration Problem." *Public Opinion,* Vol. 39 (September 30, 1906), p. 156.

384. TERESI, MATTEO. *Con la patria nel cuore; la mia propaganda fra gli emigranti.* Palermo: Casa editrice d'Antoni, 1925.

385. "To Keep Out Southern Italians," *World's Work,* v. 28 (August 1914), pp. 378-379.

386. TOMASI, SILVANO M. *An Overview of Current efforts and studies in the field of Italian immigration.* Staten Island, New York: Center for Migration Studies [*circa* 1968].

387. TOSTI, GUSTAVO. "Italy's attitude toward her emigrants," *North American Review,* v. 180 (May 1905), pp. 720-726.

388. TOSTI, GUSTAVO. *Consoli e colonie.* Philadelphia, 1906.

389. VELIKONJA, JOSEPH. "Italian Immigrants in the United States in the Mid-Sixties," *International Migration Review,* Vol I., New Series (Summer 1967), pp. 25-37.

390. VOLPE LANDI, GIOVANNI BATTISTA. "Sulla associazione detta di San Raffaele per la protezione degli emigrati italiani negli Stati Uniti," *Bollettino dell' Emigrazione* (1903).

391. VILLARI, LUIGI. *Il nazionalismo e l'emigrazione. Relazione al Congresso del Nazionalismo Italiano.* Firenze: Quattrini, 1911.

392. VILLARI, LUIGI. *Negli Stati Uniti.* Firenze: Società Nazionale Dante Alighieri, 1939.

393. VILLARI, LUIGI. "L'opinione publica Americana e i nostri emigrati," *Nuova Antologia,* V. 148 (August 1, 1910), pp. 497-517.

394. VON BOROSINI, VICTOR. "Home-going Italians," *Survey,* v. 28 (September 28, 1912), pp. 791-793.

395. WARD, ROBERT. "Italian immigration," *Outlook* (May, 1904).

396. WEINMAN, MARTHA. "Thirty-nine years, $23,000 ... then home to his wife in Italy," *Colliers,* v. 130 (July 12, 1952), pp. 62-63.

397. WEYL, BERTHA POOLE. "The heritage of the immigrant," *Outlook*, v. 89 (1908), pp. 699-704.

398. WEYL, WALTER E. "The call of America," *Outlook*, v. 94 (April 23, 1910), pp. 883-890.

399. WOLFE, BURTON. "The New Immigrants," *Sign* (September 1966), pp. 13-16. [Immigration from Italy in 1960s and the new immigration laws.]

400. ZEMA, G.A. "Italian immigrant problem," *America*, Vol. 55 (May 16, 1936), pp. 129-130.

III. ITALIAN AMERICAN HISTORY AND REGIONAL STUDIES
      A. *Comprehensive Studies*
      B. *Reminiscences, Biographies, Narratives*
      C. *Regional Studies*
         a. *Northeast*
         b. *The South*
         c. *The Midwest*
         d. *The West*

UNKNOWN PHOTOGRAPHER/ITALIAN MOTHER AND CHILD IN DINING ROOM AT ELLIS ISLAND,
c. 1905/BROWN BROTHERS

III. ITALIAN AMERICAN HISTORY [INCLUDING REMINISCENSES, BIOGRAPHIES, NARRATIVES] & REGIONAL STUDIES

There is as yet no adequate comprehensive study of the Italian experience in the United States. Despite many important books and mongraphs, no work on the experience in the United States comparable to that of Franceschini on the South American experience has as yet appeared.* In the lists that follow, ethnocentric and avowedly filiopietistic works have not been excluded since, in our view, they constitute valuable documentary and primary source materials for articulating the framework of the historiography of the Italian subcommunity. The structuring of this section has been purposely flexible to allow the listing of very varied titles within the ranges of the vast experiences of Italians in the United States.

A. Comprehensive Studies

401. ALDOVRANDI, LUIGI. *Gli Italiani negli Stati Uniti d'America.* New York, 1906.

402. CLARK, FRANCIS EDWARD. *Our Italian Fellow Citizens in Their Old Homes and Their New.* Boston: Small, Maynard, & Co., 1919.

403. GIANNOTTA, ROSARIO O. *Contributions of Italians to the development of American Culture during the eighteenth century.* Unpublished doctoral thesis, St. John's University, 1942.

404. GROSSMAN, RONALD P. *The Italians in America.* Minneapolis: Lerner Publications, 1966.

405. IORIZZO, LUCIANO J. AND SALVATORE MONDELLO, *The Italian Americans.* New York: Twayne, 1971.

406. LA PIANA, ANGELINA. *La cultura Americana e l'Italia.* Torino: G. Einaudi, 1938.

407. LOPREATO, JOSEPH. *The Italian Americans.* New York: Random House, 1970.

---

*Antonio Franceschini, *L'emigrazione italiana nell'America del Sud. Studi sull'espansione coloniale transoceanica* (Roma: Forzani, 1908).

408. LORD, ELLIOT, JOHN D. TRENNER, SAMUEL BARROWS. *The Italian in America*. New York: B.F. Buck and Company, 1906. Reprinted, San Francisco: R & E Research Associates, 1970.

409. MALNATE, NATALE. *Gli italiani in America*. Genova: Tip. Pellas, 1898.

410. MARIANO, JOHN HORACE. *The Italian contribution to American democracy*. Boston: The Christopher Publishing House, 1921. [*The second generation of Italians in New York City*. Ph.D. Thesis. New York University, 1921].

411. MONDELLO, SALVATORE ALFRED. *The Italian Immigrant in Urban America, 1880-1920, as reported in the contemporary periodical press*. Unpublished doctoral thesis, New York University, 1960.

412. MUSMANNO, MICHAEL A. *The Story of the Italians in America*, (New York: Doubleday, 1965).

413. PISANI, LAWRENCE FRANK. *The Italian in America. A social study and history*. New York: Exposition Press, 1957.

414. PREZIOSI, GIOVANNI. *Gli italiani negli Stati Uniti del Nord*. Milano: Libreria Editrice Milanese, 1909.

415. RIZZATI, FERRUCCIO. *Gli italiani in America*. Milano: Tip. Cooperativa Insubria, 1891.

416. ROLLE, ANDREW F. *The Immigrant Upraised: Italian Adventurers and Colonists in an Expanding America*. (Norman, Oklahoma: University of Oklahoma Press, 1968). Bibliography, pp. 351-371.

417. ROSE, PHILIP M. *The Italians in America*. New York: George H. Doran Co., 1922.

418. ROSSATI, G. *Gli italiani negli Stati Uniti*. New York, 1906.

419. RUGGIERO, AMERIGO. *Italiani in America*. Milano: Fratelli Treves, 1937.

420. SCHIAVO, GIOVANNI. *Four centuries of Italian-American history*. New York: Vigo Press, 1952. [2nd and 3rd eds.]

421. SCHIAVO, GIOVANNI E. *Italian-American History*. 2 vols. New York: Vigo Press, 1947-49.

422. SCHIAVO, GIOVANNI ERMENEGILDO. *Italians in America before the Civil War*. New York: G.P. Putnam's Sons, 1924. [1934]

423. TOMASI, SILVANO M. AND M.H. ENGEL, eds.   *The Italian Experience in the United States.* Staten Island, New York: Center for Migration Studies, 1970. [Includes extensive bibliographies.]

B.   *Reminiscenses, Biographies and Narratives*

424. AMBROSOLI, SOLONE.   *Partendo da New York. Versi.* Como: Franchi, 1878.

425. AQUILANO, BALDO.   *L'Ordine figli d'Italia in America. L'immigrazione italiana, 1820-1920. Le Piccole Italie. L'influenza civilo-politica' dell'ordine. America ed Americanismo. La conquista dell' L'avvenire dei Figli d'Italia.* New York: Società tipografica italiana, 1925.

426. ARRIGIONI, LEONE SANTE.   *Un Viaggio in America.* Impressioni. Torino: Tipografia Salesiana, 1906.

427. AZZARETTO, DOMENICO.   *Poesia siciliana che tratta della miseria dell'operaio in America.* Fiorenzuola d'Adda: Tipografia Pennaroli, 1908.

428. BARZINI, LUIGI.   *Americans are alone in the World.* New York: Random House, 1953. See also, *The Italians.* New York: Atheneum, 1964.

429. BERNARDY, AMY.   "Vita italiana negli Stati Uniti." *L'Italia all'estero* (Novembre - Dicembre, 1908).

430. BERNARDY, AMY A.   *Italia randagia attraverso gli Stati Uniti.* Torino: Fratelli Bocca Editori, 1913.

431. BERNARDY, AMY A.   *America vissuta.* Torino: Fratelli Bocca Editori, 1911.

432. BENANTI, SALVATORE.   *La secessione della "Sons of Italy Grand Lodge;" studi polemici su diversi problemi degl'italiani in America.* New York: Colamco Press, 1926.

433. BIAGI, ERNEST L.   *The purple aster, a history of the Order Sons of Italy in America.* New York: Veritas Publishing Co., 1961.

434. BIANCHI, ENRICO.   "L'Italiano in America," *Note e consigli* (Genova: 1925).

435. BORDONI, GIOSUÈ.   *Echi d'America: Versi.* Firenze: Tip. Claudiana, 1899.

436. BOSCO, AUGUSTO.   *Gli italiani fuori d'Italia.* Roma: Unione Tipografica Cooperativa, 1907.

437. BOSI, ALFREDO. *Cinquanti'anni di vita italiana in America.* New York: Bagnasco Press, 1921.

438. BURATTINI, ROBERTO. *Italians and Italo-Americans in Vermont.* Barre: 1931.

439. CAPUANA, LUIGI. *Gli americiani di Rabbato. Racconto.* Palermo: Sandron, 1912.

440. CAREGA DI MURICCE, FRANCESCO. *In America.* Firenze: Tip. Gazzetta d'Italia, 1875.

441. CARUSO, FILIDELFIO. *Ricordo dei benemeriti Italiani d'America.* New York: Caruso, 1908.

442. CASO, VINCENT A. *The One Hundreth Anniversary of the Arrival of Giuseppe Garibaldi in New York: In Exile from 1850-1853.* New York: New American Publishing Co., 1950.

443. CIANFARRA, CAMILLO. *Diario di un emigrante.* New York: 1900.

444. CIARLANTINI, FRANCO. *Al paese delle stelle; dall'Atlantico al Pacifico.* Milano: Edizioni "Alpes," 1931.

445. COLAJANNI, NAPOLEONE. *Gli italiani negli Stati Uniti.* Roma-Napoli: Presso la Rivista Popolare, 1910.

446. CONTE, GAETANO. *Dieci anni in America. Impressioni e ricordi.* Palermo: G. Spinnato, 1903.

447. COVELLO, LEONARD. (WITH GUIDO D'AGOSTINO). *The Heart is the Teacher.* New York: McGraw-Hill, 1958. Reprinted with *An Introduction* by F. Cordasco, New York: Littlefield & Adams, 1970 *[The Teacher in the Urban Community: A Half Century in City Schools.]*

448. CUTINO, SALVATORE. *Noi italo-americani e la storia. Lettera aperta al Prof. Giovanni Schiavo.* Milano, 1953.

449. DE AMICIS, EDMONDO. *In America.* Roma: E. Voghera, 1897.

450. DE KOSTER, PIETRO. *L'Italia e l'America.* Memorie. Genova: 1860.

451. DELITI-D'OBLIO. *Storia dell'Azione italiana negli Stati Uniti.* Roma: Tipografia l'Italiana, 1918.

452. DI SILVESTRO, GIOVANNI. *Note e appunti sulle colonie italiane negli Stati Uniti nel Nord. Relazione presentata al I Congresso delgi italiani all'estero del 1908.* Philadelphia: Tip. La Voce del Popolo, 1908.

453. EINAUDI, LUIGI. "L'italiano in America. Cio che e stato è cio che sara." *Italia Coloniale* (1900).

454. ERRIGO, JOSEPH A.L. "South Italian culture in America," *General Magazine and Historical Cronicle,* v. 37 (1935), pp. 425-430.

455. FALBO, ERNEST S., ed. [and Trans.]. Count Leonetto Cipriani, *California and Overland Diaries from 1853-1871.* Portland, Oregon: Champoeg Press, 1961.

456. FANT, P.A. *Luigi Carnovale, l'eroe della italianità negli Stati Uniti d'America.* Roma: Tip. delle Terme, 1927.

457. FERBER, NAT JOSEPH. *A new American. The life story of Salvatore A. Cotillo, Supreme Court Justice, State of New York.* New York: Farrar and Rinehart, 1938.

458. FERRARI, ROBERT. *Days pleasant and unpleasant in the Order Sons of Italy; the problem of race and racial societies in the United States. Assimilation or isolation?* New York: Mandy Press, 1926.

459. FERRERI, GHERARDO. *Gli Italiani in America; impressioni di un viaggio agli Stati Uniti.* Roma: Tipografia del Campidoglio di G. d'Antonio, 1907.

460. FOLCI, RAIMONDO. *Un viaggio negli Stati Uniti.* Palermo: Tip. Pirulla, 1914.

461. GALLENGA, ANTONIO CARLO NAPOLEONE. *Episodes of my second life. American and English experiences.* Philadelphia: J.B. Lippincott, 1885.

462. GARDINI, CARLO. *Gli Stati Uniti.* Ricordi. Bologna: Zanichelli, 1887.

463. GARLICK, RICHARD. *Philip Mazzei, Friend of Jefferson.* Baltimore: Johns Hopkins Press, 1933.

464. GIACOSA, GIUSEPPE. *Impressioni d'America.* Milano: L.F. Cogliati, 1908.

465. GROSSI, VINCENZO. "Gli Italiani negli Stati Uniti," *Rivista di sociologia* (1895).

466. GROSSI, VINCENZO. *Gli italiani in America.* Roma: Tipografia di G. Balbi, 1896. (Reprinted from *L'Economista d'Italia,* no. 30, 31, 32, 33, 34, [Luglio - Agosto 1896].

467. H., G. "Gli italiani negli Stati Uniti," *L'Italia coloniale,* v. 2 (September 1901), pp. 87-90.

468. IAMURRI, GABRIEL A. *The true story of an immigrant.* Rev. ed. Boston: Christopher Publishing House, 1951.

469. *IL PROBLEMA ITALIANO NEGLI STATI UNITI.* Pesaro: Tip. Interenzi, 1909.

470. LANDOLFI, AMALIO. *La mia strenua propaganda all'estero (1925-1926).* Avellino: Premiata tipografia pergola, 1926.

471. LO GRASSO, ANGELINE H. *Piero Marconelli.* Roma: Atenco, 1958.

472. LUSSANA, FILIPPO. *Lettere di Illetterati.* Bologna, 1913.

473. MAFFEI, GIOCCHINO. *L'Italia nell'America del Nord; rilievi e suggerimenti per la grandezza e per l'onore d'Italia.* Valle di Pompei: F. Sicignano & Co., 1924.

474. MARRARO, H.R. "Garibaldi in New York," *New York History* (1934).

475. MARRARO, H.R. "Lincoln's Italian Volunteers from New York," *New York History* (April 1946).

476. MAZZEI, PHILIP. *Memoirs.* Trans. by H.R. Marraro. New York: Columbia University Press, 1942.

477. NICOTRI, GASPARE. *Dalla Conca d'Oro all' 'Golden Gate'; studi e impressioni di viaggio in America.* New York: Canorna Press, 1928.

478. NEIDLE, CECYLE S., *The New Americans* New York: Twayne, 1967. Includes notices of Leonard Covello, Angelo Pellegrini, Constantine Nunzio, Edward Corsi and Pascal d'Angelo.

479. PANUNZIO, CONSTANTINE M. *Immigrant crossroads.* New York: The Macmillan Co., 1927.

480. PANUNZIO, CONSTANTINE M. *The immigrant portrayed in biography and story: a selected list with notes.* New York: Foreign Language Information Service, 1925.

481. PANUNZIO, CONSTANTINE M.   *The soul of an immigrant.* New York: The Macmillan Co., 1922. [1924; 1934]

482. PEEBLES, ROBERT.   *Leonard Covello: An Immigrant's Contribution to New York City.* Unpublished doctoral thesis, New York University, 1967.

483. PELLEGRINI, ANGELO M.   *Immigrant's return.* New York: Macmillan, 1951.

484. PELLEGRINI, ANGELO M.   *American by choice.* New York: Macmillan, 1956.

485. [POPE, GENEROSO.]   "Americanization of Mr. Pope," *Time,* vol. 38 (September 22, 1941), p. 57.

486. [POPE, FORTUNE.]   "Portrait," *Fortune,* vol. 22 (November 1940), p. 86.

487. PREZZOLINI, GIUSEPPE.   *America in pantofole: un impero senza imperialisti. Ragguagli intorno alla transformazione degli Stati Uniti dopo le guerre mondiali.* Firenze: Valecchi, 1950.

488. PREZZOLINI, G.   *L'Italiano inutile.* Milano: Longanesi, 1953. [Parte Terza: "America," pp. 223-359.]

489. PUCELLI, RODOLFO.   *Sonetti biografici di italo-americani.* Milano: Castaldi, 1950.

490. RATTO, MARIO ORSINI.   *L'avvenire degli italo-americani.* Milano: Fratelli Treves, 1933.

491. RIDOLFI, LUIGI.   *Quadri e cuori.* Udine: Arti grafiche friulane, 1948.

492. ROSELLI, BRUNO.   *Francesco Vigo: Italiano d'America, 1747-1836.* Roma: Segret. faci italiani all'estera, 1932.

493. ROSSI, ADOLFO.   *Vita d'America.* Roma: E. Perino, 1891.

494. ROSSI, ADOLFO.   *Un italiano in America.* Con uno studio biografico di Bernardo Chiara. Treviso: L. Buffetti, 1907. [originally, 1891]

495. ROSSI, ADOLFO.   *Nel paese dei dollari [Tre anni a New York].* Milano: Kantorvinz, 1893.

496. ROSSI, ADOLFO.   *Impressioni italo-americane.* Roma: Unione Tipografica Cooperativa, 1907.

497. ROSSI, JOSEPH.   "The myth of the Italian Risorgimento: The letters from America of Carlo Vidua," *Italica,* vol. 38 (1961), pp. 227-35.

498. RUGGIERO, AMERIGO. *Italiani in America.* Milano: Treves, 1939.

499. SANTINI, FLORIO. *Figli d'Italia in America.* Lucca: Villaggio del Fanciullo, 1958.

500. SANTORO, DANIEL AND JOHN A. RALLO, *Italians-past and present.* New York: Staten Island Italian Historical Society, 1955.

501. SICILIANI, DOMENICO. *Fra gli italiani degli Stati Uniti d'America* [Luglio-Settembre 1921]. Roma· Stabilimento poligrafico per l'amministrazione della guerra, 1922.

502. SOLDATI, MARIO. *America, primo amore!* [Saggi]. Roma: G. Einaudi, 1945. Also published as *Amerique, premier amour.* Paris: Editions de portes de France, 1947.

503. SPADONI, ADRIANA. "A great man: the second of three stories of Italian life in America," *Outlook,* v. 104 (July 26, 1913), pp. 684-691.

504. SPERANZA, GINO C. *The Diary of Gino Speranza, Italy, 1915-1919.* Edited by Florence Colgate Speranza. New York: Columbia University Press, 1941. 2 vols. [Gino Charles Speranza, 1872-1927].

505. STRAFFILE, ALFONSO. *Memorandum coloniale ossia sintesi storica di osservazioni e fatti che diano un'idea generale della vita coloniale degli Italiani nel Nord America.* Philadelphia: Tip. La Forbice, 1911.

506. *STUDI E RICERCHE DI STORIA DI SICILIA.* *Con un' appendice di saggi italo-Americani.* (Padova, 1963).

507. TORIELLI, ANDREW JOSEPH. *Italian opinion on America as revealed by Italian travelers, 1850-1900.* Cambridge, Mass.: Harvard University Press, 1941.

508. TUONI, G.M. *Attività italiana in America.* San Francisco, 1930.

509. VENTRASCA, FRANCESCO. *Personal Reminiscences of a naturalized American.* New York: Daniel Rueson, 1937.

510. VILLARI, LUIGI. *Negli Stati Uniti.* Società Nazionale Dante Alighieri, 1939.

511. VILLARI, LUIGI. *Gli italiani negli Stati Uniti.* Roma: Palazzo Antici-Mattei, 1939.

512. VILLARI, LUIGI. "Gli italiani d'America ieri e oggi," *Nuova Antologia,* v. 394. (December 1, 1937), pp. 282-287.

513. ZAGNONI, AUTERO. *Pro veritate. Alcune lettere sulla colonia italiana di New York.* New York: Tip. Aste, 1900.

C.   *Regional Studies*

a.   Northeast

514. ACCARDI, LEONARD. *Italian Contribution to Albany in the Nineteenth Century.* Schenectady, New York: Franklin, 1941.

515. ACRITELLI, PIETRO. "In contributo degli Italiani alla prosperità materiale della città di New York," *L'Italia coloniale,* vol. 1 (January - February, 1904), pp. 36-40.

516. ADAMS, CHARLOTTE. "Italian life in New York," *Harper's Monthly,* v. 62, no. 371 (April, 1881), pp. 666-684.

517. ADAMS, C. G. "On the roofs of the Latin quarter," *Overland Monthly,* n.s. 57 (1911), p. 330.

518. ALDOVRANDI, LUIGI. "Note sull'emigrazione italiana in Pennsylvania," *Bollettino dell'emigrazione* (1911).

519. ALTARELLI, CARLO C. *History and present conditions of the Italian colony at Paterson, N.J.* New York: Columbia University Studies in Sociology, 1911.

520. AQUILANO, BALDO. *Gli Italiani nel Long Island.* Con prefazione di T. Roosevelt. New York: 1911.

521. BARRESE, PAULINE J. "Southern Italian Folklore in New York City," *New York Folklore Quarterly,* XXI (September 1965), pp. 181-193.

522. BEETS, LILLIAN. "Italian peasants in a new law tenement," *Harper's Bazar,* v. 38 (August, 1904), pp. 802-805.

523. BENELLI, G.P. "Gli Italiani in alcuni distretti dello stato di New York," *Bollettino dell'Emigrazione* (1902).

524. BERNARDY, AMY. *Piccola Italia.* Firenze: Galileiana, 1906.

525. BETTS, LILLIAN W. *The Italian in New York.* New York: University Settlement Studies, 1904-1905.

526. BIAGI, ERNESTO L. *The Italians of Philadelphia.* New York, 1967.

527.. BRACE, CHARLES LORING. *The Dangerous Classes of New York.* New York: Wynkoop & Hallenbeck, 1872 [Notice of Italians in N.Y.C.]

528. BUSHÉE, FREDERICK A. "Italian immigrants in Boston," *Arena*, v. 17 (1897), pp. 722-734.

529. CARLEVALE, JOSEPH WILLIAM. *Americans of Italian descent in New Jersey*. Clifton, N.J.: North Jersey Press, 1950.

530. CARLEVALE, JOSEPH WILLIAM. *American of Italian descent in Philadelphia and vicinity, including Wilmington, Del.: Distinguished Americans of Italian descent in Greater Philadelphia who are making a significant contribution in their chosen vocation*. Philadelphia: G.S. Ferguson Company, 1954.

531. CARLEVALE, JOSEPH WILLIAMS. *Leading Americans of Italian descent in Massachusetts*. Plymouth, Mass.: Printed by the Memorial Press, 1946.

532. CARLEVALE, JOSEPH WILLIAM. *Who's who among Americans of Italian descent in Connecticut*. New Haven: Carlevale Publishing Company, 1942.

533. CHURCHILL, CHARLES WESLEY. *The Italians of Newark: A Community Study*. New York: New York University, 1946. [Ph.D. dissertation. New York University. Graduate School of Arts and Sciences, 1942].

534. CONGRESSO DEGLI ITALIANI ALL'ESTERO. Roma, 1908. Comitato coloniale locale del Connecticut. Stato di Connecticut, U.S.A. *Relazione del comitato coloniale per il congresso*. Redate e stampata per cura della Società italiane di Stamford, Conn.

535. CONTE, A. "La protezione degli immigrati italiani in Boston," *Bollettino dell'Emigrazione* (1903).

536. COOKE, HARRIET T. "An Italian Colony," *Survey*, v. 45 (November 20, 1920), pp. 277-278.

537. CORDASCO, F. and R. GALATTIOTO. "Ethnic Displacement in the Interstitial Community: The East Harlem [New York City] Experience," *Phylon: The Atlanta University Review of Race & Culture*, vol. 31 (Fall 1970), pp. 302-312; also in *Journal of Negro Education*, vol. 40 (Winter 1971), pp. 56-65. [Notices of the Italian community.]

538. CORDASCO, F. *Jacob Riis Revisited: Poverty and the Slum in Another Era*. New York: Doubleday, 1968. [Italians in New York. Riis' photographs of the Italian subcommunity in New York City (1890-1905?) are in the Jacob A. Riis Collection, Museum of the City of New York.]

539. CORNWELL, E.E., Jr. "Party absorption of ethnic group; the case of Providence, Rhode Island," *Social Forces,* v. 38 (March 1960), pp. 205-210.

540. CORSI, EDWARD, "My Neighborhood," *Outlook,* vol. 141 (September 16, 1925), pp. 90-91.

541. CUSUMANO, GASPARE. *Study of the colony of Cinisi in New York City.* [Unpublished manuscript]

542. DALL'ASTE-BRANDOLINI, ANGELO. "L'immigrazione e le colonie italiane nella Pennsylvania," *Bollettino dell'Emigrazione* (1902).

543. DAVENPORT, WILLIAM E. *Beggarman of Brooklyn Heights, and other chants. With the Italian settlement.* Brooklyn, 1904.

544. DeBIASI, M. "Colonie italiane d'America: Philadelphia," *L'Italia coloniale,* v. 1 (January - February, 1904), pp. 48-58.

545. *Di PALMA DI CASTIGLIONE, G.E. "L'Ufficio del lavoro per emigranti in New York," *Bollettino dell'Emigrazione* (1909).

546. "Festa; festival of San Gennaro, New York City," *New Yorker,* v. 33 (October 5, 1957), pp. 34-36.

547. FRANZONI, A. *Gli interessi italiani in New York.* Roma, 1908.

548. FRY, HORACE B. *Little Italy.* A tragedy in one act. New York: R.H. Russell, 1902.

549. GERTRUDE, AGNES, SR. "Italian Immigrants into Philadelphia," *American Catholic Historical Society Records,* Vol. 58 (June-December, 1947) pp. 133-143; 189-208; 256-257.

550. GIACOSA, GIUSEPPE. "Gli italiani a New York ed a Chicago," *Nuova Antologia,* v. 124 (August 16, 1892), pp. 618-640.

551. HILLARD, MARY H. "The Italians in New England," *Bulletin and Italiana* (Italy America Society), v. 1 (November 1927), pp. 1-4.

552. HOWE, MAUDE. "From Italy to Pittsburgh: where the Pennsylvania Italians come from," *Lippincott's Monthly Magazine,* v. 73, (February 1904), pp. 200-208.

553. HOWELLS, WILLIAM DEAN. *Suburban Sketches,* (Cambridge: Houghton Miflin, 1870). [Chapter entitled "Doorstep Acquaintance," pp. 35-59, on Italians in Boston area.]

554. IRWIN, GRACE. "Michelangelo in Newark," *Harper's Magazine,* v. 143 (September 1921), pp. 446-454.

*Name also appears as G. E. Di P. Castiglione.

555. "Italian festivals in New York," *Chautauquan,* v. 34 (1901), pp. 228-229.

556. "Italians in Boston," *Charities,* v. 12 (1904), pp. 451-452.

557. *ITALIANS IN NEW YORK CITY.* Report. U.S. Industrial Commission, v. 15, pp. 473-492.

558. KAPP, F. *L'Emigrazione New York.* [1870]

559. KNEPLER, ABRAHAM E., ed. *The Columbus day booklet.* Bridgeport: University of Bridgeport, Colloquium, 1950.

560. "(LA) Society For Italian Immigrants E La Casa Per Gli Italiani in New York," *Bollettino dell'Emigrazione* (1912).

561. "Little Italy in the streets of Paul Revere," *Independent,* v. 114 (June 20, 1925), pp. 696-694.

562. LUBELL, SAMUEL. "Rhode Island's little firecrackers," *Saturday Evening Post,* v. 222 (November 12, 1949) pp. 31 174-178.

563. LYNCH, BERNARD J. "The Italians in New York," *Catholic World,* v. 47, no. 277 (April 1888), p. 67-73.

564. MAINIERO, JOSEPH. *History of the Italians in Trenton, New Jersey.* Trenton: Commercial Printing Col, 1929.

565. MANGANO, ANTONIO. *Italian colonies in New York City.* New York: Columbia University Studies in Sociology, 1904.

566. MANSON, GEORGE J. "The foreign element in New York City. V: The Italians," *Harper's Weekly,* v. 34 (October 18, 1890), pp. 817-820.

567. MARRARO, HOWARD R. "Italo-Americans in eighteenth-century New York," *New York History,* v. 21 (July, 1940), pp. 316-323.

568. MARRARO, HOWARD R. "Italo-Americans in Pennsylvania in the eighteenth century," *Pennsylvania History,* v. 7 (1940), pp. 159-166.

569. MARRARO, HOWARD R. "Italians in New York during the first half of the nineteenth century," *New York History,* v. 26 (July 1945), pp. 278-306.

570. MARRARO, HOWARD R. "Italians in New York in the eighteen fifties," *New York History,* v. 30 (April - July, 1949), pp. 181-203, 276-303.

571. McCARTY, JOSEPH. "A Little Italy along the banks of the Merrimac," *New England Magazine,* n.s., v. 41 (1909), pp. 832-835.

572. McKELVEY, BLAKE. "The Italians of Rochester: An Historical Review," *Rochester History*, vol. 22, (1960). See also, Matteo Teresi. *Memoriale della American Italian Union di Rochester, N.Y. al Congresso Coloniale di Roma*. Buffalo: Tip. del Risveglio, 1908.

573. MIGLIORE, SALVATORE. *Half a century of Italian immigration into Pittsburgh and Allegheny County*. [Unpublished Master's thesis, University of Pittsburgh, 1928]

574. MOFFAT, ADELENE. "Exhibition of Italian arts and crafts in Boston," *Survey*, v. 22 (1909), pp. 51-53.

575. "Mulberry bend from 1897 to 1958," *Saturday Evening Post*, v. 231 (August 2, 1958), pp. 34-35.

576. NASELLI, G. "Gli italiani nel distretto consolare di Filadelfia," *Bollettino dell'Emigrazione* (1903).

577. "New York's Italians: A Question of Identity Within and Without," *New York Times*, November 9, 1970.

578. "Operai italiani nel Connecticut," *Bollettino del Ministero Degli Affari Esteri* (Febbràio 1896).

579. ORDER OF SONS OF ITALY IN AMERICA. New York [City]. Loggia Alessandro Manzoni, No. 381. *Statuto e regolamento interno della Loggia Alessandro Manzoni, No. 381. ...di New York*. New York: Soc. Tipografica Italiana, 1915.

580. PAPA, DARIO-FONTANA. *New York*. Milano: Galli, 1884.

581. PERRY, G.S. "Omaricos of New Haven," *Saturday Evening Post*, v. 221 (1948), pp. 28-29.

582. PESATURO, UBALDO U.M. *The Italo-Americans in Rhode Island, their contributions and achievements*. Providence, R.I.: 1937.

583. PESATURO, UBALDO U.M. *Italo-Americans of Rhode Island; an historical and biographical survey of the origin, rise and progress of Rhode Islanders of Italian birth and descent*. 2nd. edition. Providence, R.I.: Visitor Printing Co., 1940.

584. PILEGGI, NICHOLAS, "Little Italy: Study of an Italian Ghetto," *New York*, Vol. 1 (August 12, 1968), pp. 14-23.

585. *PROGRESSO. Italo Americano di New York. Monografia*. New York: Nicoletti Bros. Press, 1911.

586. PYRKE, BERNE A. *Long Island's first Italian, 1639.* Amityville, 1943. (Reprinted from the *Long Island Forum.*)

587. *Relazione del I e II Congresso degli Italiani neglie Stati Uniti. Philadelphia, Pa., 1911 - Buffalo, N.Y., 1912. Formazione e Regolamento dell'Alleanza italo-americana degli Stati Uniti d'America.* Philadelphia, Pa.: Nardiello, Press, 1913.

588. RIIS, JACOB A. "Feast-days in Little Italy," *Century,* v. 58 (August, 1899), pp. 491-499.

589. RIIS, JACOB A. "The Italian in New York," *How the other half lives. Studies among the tenements of New York.* New York: Charles Scribner's Sons, 1890.

590. ROSEBORO, VIOLA. "The Italians of New York," *Cosmopolitan,* v. 4 (January, 1888), pp. 396-406.

591. ROSSATI, G. "Organizzazione e opera dell'Ufficio di Collocamento al lavoro in New York per gli emigranti italiani," *Bollettino dell'Emigrazione* (1907).

592. SARTORIS, ANTONIO. "Fra gli Italiani emigrati nella Pennsylvania," *Italica Gens,* v. 6 (1915), pp. 132-135.

593. SCHIRO, GEORGE. *Americans by Choice.* [History of the Italians in Utica]. Utica, N.Y.: Thomas J. Griffith Sons, Inc., 1940.

594. SCUDDER, VIDA. "Experiments in fellowship work with Italians in Boston," *Survey,* v. 22 (1909), pp. 47-51.

595. SHEDD, WILLIAM B. 'Italian population in New York City. *The Casa Italiana Educational Bureau,* Bulletin No. 7 (1934); [Also published in *Atlantica,* September 1934].

596. SIMMONDS, D.C. "Anti-Italian American Riddles in New England," *Journal of American Folklore,* vol. 79 (July 1966), pp. 425-478.

597. [Sister] M. AGNES GERTRUDE. "Italian immigration into Philadelphia," *American Catholic Historical Society of Philadelphia Records* v. 58 (1947), pp. 133-143, 189-208, 256-257.

598. SPEED, J. GILMER. "The Mulberry Bend," *Harper's Weekly,* v. 36 (April 30, 1892), p. 430.

599. STAFFFILE, ALFONSO. *Memorandum coloniale con monografia illustrativa della colonia di Filadelfia.* Philadelphia, Pa.: Tip. Mastro Antonio, 1910.

600. THAON Di REVEL, VITTORIO.   "Rapporto circa l'emigrazione italiana nel distretto consolare di Boston," *Bollettino del Ministero degli Affari Esteri* (1889).

601. TISCARO, I.   "L'emigrazione italiana nel distretto di Scranton, Penn." *Bollettino dell'Emigrazione* (1913).

602. TOMANIO, ANTHONY J. and LUCILLE N. LaMACCHIA.   *The Italian-American Community in Bridgeport.* Bridgeport, Conn.: University of Bridgeport Community Area Study. Student Monograph. No. 5 (1953).

603. TOMASI, MARI.   "The Italian story in Vermont," *Vermont History* (Burlington), v. 28. (January 1960), pp. 73-87.

604. U.S. Federal Writer's Project. New York City. *THE ITALIANS OF NEW YORK.* A survey prepared by workers of the Federal Writer's Project. Work Progress Administration in the City of New York. New York: Random House, 1938. [Published also in Italian]

605. VECOLI, RUDOLPH J.   *The People of New Jersey,* Princeton: Van Nostrand, 1965. [Chapter on Italians.]

606. VILLARI, LUIGI.   "L'emigrazione italiana nel distretto consolare di Filadelfia," *Bollettino dell' Emigrazione* (1908).

607. WHELAN, ANNE.   "The romance of the Italians in Bridgeport," *The Bridgeport Post,* October 8, 1934.

608. WOODS, AMY.   "Italians of New England," *New England Magazine,* v. 30 (July 1904), pp. 626-632.

609. WOODS, ROBERT A.   "Notes on the Italians in Boston," *Charities,* v. 12 (May 7, 1904), pp. 541-542.

C.   *Regional Studies*

b.   The South

610. AARONSON, R.R.   "Pecan Tree," *Common Ground,* Vol. 10, No. 1
      (1949), pp. 75-88. [Sicilians in New Orleans].

611. "A model Italian colony in Arkansas," *Review Of Reviews,* v 34 (September 1906), pp. 361-362.

612. BRANDFON, ROBERT L.   "The End of Immigration to the Cotton
      Fields," *The Mississippi Valley Historical Review,* vol. 50 (March 1964), p.
      591-611. [On attempts to replace Negroes with Italian agricultural
      workers.]

613. CARACHRIST, C.F.Z.   "Italian immigration to the South." *Manufacturers' Record,* (August 1905).

614. CHIESI, GUSTAVO.   *La nostra emigrazione negli Stati Uniti e la
      colonizzazione italiana nel Texas.* Roma: Unione Tipografica Cooperativa,
      1908.

615. CLARK, ELMER TALMAGE.   *The Latin immigrant in the South.*
      Nashville: The Cokesbury Press, 1924.

616. COMPAGNONI-MEREFOSCHI, MARIO.   "Notizie sulla Luisiana."
      Bollettino Consolare (Marzo-Aprile 1884).

617. CORTE, PASQUALE.   La colonia italiana negli Stati Uniti del Texas,
      Mississippi, Florida, Alabama, Arkansas, e Luigiana. Rapporto del cav. avv.
      P. Corte, R. Console a Nuova Orleans," *Bollettino del Ministero degli Affari
      Esteri* (1891).

618. CUNNINGHAM, G.E.   "Italians: a hindrance to white solidarity in
      Louisiana, 1890-1898," *Journal of Negro History,* vol. 50 (January 1965),
      pp. 22-36.

619. DES PLANCHES, EDMONDO.   "Nel Sud degli Stati Uniti," *Nuova
      Antologia,* v. 206 (16 February - March, 1906), pp. 593-615, 3-30.
      [Published also in: *Rassegna Nazionale*]

620. FERRERO, FELICE.   "A new St. Helena," *Survey,* v. 23 (November 6,
      1909), pp. 171-180.

621. FLEMING, WALTER F.   "Immigration to the Southern States," *Political
      Science Quarterly,* v. 20, (June 1905), pp. 276-297. [Italians, pp. 292-296].

622. HEWES, LESLIE. "Tontitown: Ozark Vineyard Center [features of the predominately Italian community and how it developed]," *Economic Geography*, vol. 29 (April 1953), pp. 125-143.

623. "Italian Exile in America," *Southern Literary Messenger*, vol. 8 (1842), p. 741.

624. "Italians in the South;" "The South wants Italians," *Outlook*, v. 87 (1907), pp. 556-558.

625. LANGLEY, LEE J. "Italian as a southern farmer. Striking characterization of their success and value to the community," *Manufacturers' Record* (August 1904).

626. LANGLEY, LEE J. "Italians in cotton field. Their superiority over Negroes shown on an Arkansas Plantation," *Manufacturers' Record*, (April 1904).

627. MEADE, EMILY FOGG. "Italian immigration into the South," *South Atlantic Quarterly*, v. 4 (July 1905), pp. 217-223.

628. MORONI, G. "L'emigrazione italiana nel distretto di New Orleans," *Bollettino dell'Emigrazione* (1908).

629. MORONI, G. "Società italiane nel distretto consolare di New Orleans," *Bollettino dell'Emigrazione* (1910).

630. MORONI, G. "La Luisiana e l'emigrazione italiana," *Bollettino dell'Emigrazione* (1913).

631. MORONI, G. "L'emigrazione italiana in Florida," *Bollettino dell'Emigrazione* (1913).

632. PAPINI, C. "Gli Stati di Luisiana, Texas, Florida, e Mississippi," *Bollettino del Ministero degli Affari Esteri* (1895).

633. PHENIS, ALBERT. "Italian immigration to the South," *Manufacturers' Record* (May 1905).

634. *Progetto di colonizzazione nell'Alabama, U.S.A.* Roma: Tip. Archivio Clinico Italiano, 1880.

635. SADA, LUIGI. *Progetto di società commerciale per la protezione dell'industria in conseguenza della colonizzazione italiana del Texas.* Milano: Tip. Colombi e Cordani, 1881.

636. SAINT MARTIN, G. "Gli Italiani nel distretto consolare di New Orleans, Louisiana, Texas, Florida, Mississippi," *Bollettino dell'Emigrazione* (1903).

637. SCALA, LUIGI. *Poche considerazioni sull'emigrazione italiana negli Stati Uniti e particolarmente in Louisiana.* Roma, 1911.

638. RAMIREZ, M.D. "Italian Folklore from Tampa, Florida," *Southern Folklore Quarterly,* vol. 13 (June 1949), pp. 121-132; also, pp. 101-106.

639. ROSSATI, G. "La colonizzazione negli stati di Mississippi, Louisiana, ed Alabama." *Bollettino dell'Emigrazione,* (1904).

640. ROSELLI, BRUNO. *Let the dead speak!* Poughkeepsie, N.Y.. Artcraft Press, 1929, [Tombstone inscriptions, New Orleans.]

641. ROSELLI, BRUNO. *The Italians in colonial Florida: a repertory of Italian families settled in Florida under Spanish (1513-1762; 1784-1821) and British (1762–1784) regimes.* Jacksonville, Fla.: Drew Press, 1940.

642. VILLARI, LUIGI. "Gli Italiani nel Sud degli Stati Uniti," *Bollettino dell'Emigrazione,* (1907).

C.   *Regional Studies*

c.   Midwest

643. BECK, FRANK ORMAN.   "The Italians in Chicago," *City of Chicago*. City of Chicago. Department of Public Welfare. *Bulletin*, v. 2 (February 1919), pp. 5-32.

644. BOYER, BRIAN,   "Chicago's Italians," *Midwest*, [Chicago Sun Times] (July 14, 1968), p. 6+

645. CANCE, ALEXANDER E.   "Piedmontese on the Mississippi," *Survey*, v. 26 (September 2, 1911), pp. 779-785.

646. CASTIGLIONE, A.   "Origine e sviluppo, importanza e avvenire delle colonie italiane nel Nord Michigan e nel Nord Minnesota," *Bollettino dell'Emigrazione* (1913).

647. CASTIGLIONE, G.E. Di P.   "Numero, provenienza e distribuzione degli italiani residenti in Chicago," *Bollettino dell'Emigrazione*, (1915).

648. CASTIGLIONE, G.E. Di P.   "Vari centri italiani negli Stati di Indiana, Ohio, Minnesota, Wisconsin," *Bollettino dell'Emigrazione*, (1915).

649. CIPRIANI, LISI.   *Selected directory of the Italians in Chicago. Market guide and yearly information bulletin*. Chicago: 1927.

650. CIPRIANI, LISI.   *Italians in Chicago and the selected directory of the Italians in Chicago*. Chicago: 1933.

651. COULTER, CHARLES WELLESLEY.   *The Italians of Cleveland*. Cleveland: Cleveland Americanization Committee. Mayor's Advisory War Committee, 1919.

652. DUNNE, EDMUND M.   "Memoirs of 'Zi Pre' [Among the Italians in Chicago]," *Ecclesiastic Review*, v. 49 (1913), pp. 192-203.

653. FIORE, ALPHONSE THOMAS.   *History of Italian Immigration in Nebraska*. Lincoln, Nebraska: University of Nebraska, 1942. [Ph.D. thesis, 1938].

654. GIACOSA, GIUSEPPE.   "Chicago e la sua colonia," *Nuova Antologia*, v. 124 (March 1, 1893), pp. 15-33.

655. "Greeks and Italians in the Neighborhood of the Hull House," *American Journal of Sociology*, vol. XXI (November, 1915), pp. 285-316.

656. "Italians in Chicago," *Municipal Affairs*, v. 1 (1897), 777-778.

657. *Italians in Chicago: social and ecomomic study*, Superintendent of Documents, 1894.

658. "Italians in Chicago: the rise of an immigrant community," *The Interpreter*, v. 8 (September 1929), pp. 107-112.

659. "Italians in Madison, Wis. Truth about Columbus Park," *Wisconsin State Journal*, March 21-31, 1929 [series of articles].

660. La PIANA, GEORGE. *The Italians in Milwaukee, Wisconsin: General survey, prepared under the direction of the Associated Charities.* Milwaukee, Wis.: 1915. Reprinted, San Francisco: R & E Research Associates, 1970.

661. LEAVITT, MARIE. *Report on the Sicilian colony in Chicago.* [Unpublished Manuscript]. University of Chicago Library.

662. MANFREDINI, DOLORES M. "The Italians come to Herrin," *Illinois State Historical Society.* Journal. v. 37 (December 1944), pp. 317-328.

663. MASTRO-VALERIO, ALESSANDRO. "Remarks upon the Italian colony in Chicago," *Hull House Maps and Papers.* A presentation of nationalities and wages in a congested district of Chicago, together with comments and essays on problems growing out of the social conditions, by residents of Hull House, a social settlement at 235 South Halstead Street, Chicago, Ill. New York. Boston: T.Y. Crowell & Co., 1895.

664. NELLI, HUMBERT S. *The Italians in Chicago: A Study in Ethnic Mobility.* New York: Oxford University Press, 1970. [Considerable documentation and bibliographies.]

665. NORTON, GRACE P. "Chicago Housing conditions. VII. Two Italian districts," *American Journal of Sociology*, v. 18 (1913), pp. 509-542. (published also in: Sophonisba Breckenridge, ed. *The Housing problem of Chicago.* Chicago: The University of Chicago Press, 1910-1915.)

666. PITTS, G.L. "Italians of Columbus, Ohio. A study in population," *Annals, American Academy of Political and Social Science*, v. 19 (1902), pp. 154-159.

667. PRINDIVILLE, KATE G. "Italy in Chicago," *Catholic World*, v. 77 (July, 1903), pp. 452-461.

668. PROVANA DEL SABBIONE, L. "Le condizioni nel disretto consolare di Chicago," *Bollettino dell'Emigrazione* (1913).

669. PUZZO, VIRGIL PETER. *The Italians in Chicago, 1890-1930.* [Unpublished M.A. thesis, University of Chicago (History), 1937.]

670. QUAINTANCE, ESTHER CROCKETT. *Rent and housing conditions in the Italian district of the Lower North Side of Chicago.* [Unpublished M.A. thesis, University of Chicago, School of Social Service Administration]

671. RANKIN, LOIS. "Detroit nationality groups," *Michigan History Magazine,* v. 23 (1939), pp. 129-205.

672. SAGER, GERTRUDE AILEEN. *Immigration: based upon a study of the Italian women and girls of Chicago.* [Unpublished M.A. thesis, University of Chicago (Sociology), 1914]

673. SCHIAVO, GIOVANNI. *The Italians in Chicago: a study in Americanization.* Chicago: Italian American Publishing Company, 1928.

674. SCHIAVO, GIOVANNI. *The Italians in Missouri.* Chicago: Italian American Publishing Co., 1929.

675. Società Unione e Fratellanza Italiana. *Seventy-fifth Anniversary.* Diamond jubilee of the Società; historical review; chronological history of Fratellanza; brief history of Italians in the world, in the United States, in St. Louis. Banquet at York Hotel, November 9, 1941. St. Louis, 1941.

676. "Stranger in Emoria," *Literary Digest,* v. 50 (April 17, 1915), p. 901.

677. U.S. BUREAU OF LABOR. *The Italians in Chicago.* A social and economic study. Ninth Special Report of the Commissioner of Labor. Prepared under the direction of Caroll D. Wright. Washington, D.C.: Government Printing Office, 1897.

678. VECOLI, RUDOLPH J. *Chicago's Italians Prior to World War I: A Study of their Social and Economic adjustment.* [Unpublished doctoral thesis. University of Wisconsin, 1963.]

679. VECOLI, RUDOLPH J. "Contadini in Chicago: a critique of *The Uprooted,*" *Journal of American History,* vol. 51 (December 1964), pp. 404-417.

680. VISMARA, JOHN C. "The coming of the Italians to Detroit," *Michigan History Magazine,* v. 11 (January 1918), pp. 110-124.

681. "The Chicago Housing conditions, 1900-1905," *Charities,* v. 15 (January 6, 1905), pp. 455-461.

682. WALKER, NATALIE. "Chicago housing conditions. X. Greeks and Italians in the neighborhood of Hull House," *American Journal of Sociology,* v. 21 (November 1915), pp. 285-316. Also published in Sophonisba Breckinridge, ed., *The housing problem of Chicago.* Chicago: The University of Chicago Press, 1910-1915.

683. WRITERS' PROGRAM [Nebraska]. *The Italians of Omaha.* Omaha: Independent Printing Co., 1941.

C.   *Regional Studies*

d.   The West

684. ABATE, P.B.   "Stato di California." *Bollettino Consolare* (1863).

685. BARELA, ATTILIO.   "L'emigrazione italiana e la California," *Italia coloniale* (1904).

686. BERNARDY, AMY.   "La colonia italiana di Los Angeles," *Cal. Rivista Coloniale,* (Settembre, 1913).

687. BOHME, FREDERICK, G.   *A History of the Italians in New Mexico.* [Unpublished doctoral thesis, University of New Mexico, 1958.]

688. BOHME, FREDERICK G.   "The Italians in New Mexico," *New Mexico Historical Review* (April 1959), pp. 98-116.

689. BONARDELLI, EUGENIO.   *Emigrazione e colonizzazione italiana nella costa del Pacifico.* Firenze: Tipografia Rassegna Nazionale, 1912.

690. BRANCHI, CAMILLO.   "Gli italiani nella storia dell California," *L'Universo,* (May-June, 1956), pp. 421-432.

691. BRENNA, PAOLO.   "Interessi dell'emigrazione italiana negli stati di Washington, Oregon, Idaho, e Montana." *Bollettino dell'Emigrazione* (1916).

692. CERRUTI, G.B.   "Sulla colonia italiana in California," *Rapporto. Bollettino Consolare.* (Luglio 1871).

693. CASAMORATA, CESARE.   "In California," *L'Universo* (1920), pp. 321-334.

694. "Condizioni delle colonie italiane a Stockton e nelle contee di Sonora, Jackson e Amador City (Cal.)," *Bollettino dell'Emigrazione* (1915).

695. "Congresso dell'immigrazione della Costa del Pacifico," *Bollettino dell'Emigrazione* (1913).

696. CRESPI, CESARE.   *San Francisco e la sua catastrofe.* San Francisco, Tipografia internazionale, 1906.

697. CUNEO, G.   "L'immigrazione italiana nel Colorado e nell' Utah." *Bollettino dell'Emigrazione* (1902).

698. DES PLANCHES, EDMONDO. *California. Gil Italiani in California.* Roma: Tipografia del Ministero degli Affari Esteri, 1904, [Reprinted from *Bollettino del Ministero degli Affari Esteri,* February, 1904.]

699. DONDERO, C. "L'Italia negli Stati Uniti ed in California," *L'Italia coloniale,* v. 1 (June 1901), pp. 9-22.

700. "Emigrazione italiana e la California." *Italia Coloniale* (Aprile - Maggio 1903).

701. FRANGINI, A. *Italiani in San Francisco e Oakland, Cal. Cenni biografici.* San Francisco: Tipografia Lanson-Lauray, 1914.

702. "Gli Italiani in California e negli Stati della costa del Pacifico," *Bollettino dell'Emigrazione* (1902).

703. *Guida generale italiana della contea di San Joaquin. Calestini's Italian commercial and residential directory, Stockton.* Stockton: L. Calestini, 1915.

704. "Italians in California," *The Interpreter,* v. 7 (January 1928), pp. 12-14.

705. JONES, IDWAL. "Evviva San Francisco," *American Mercury,* v. 12 (October 1927), pp. 151-158.

706. *LA VOCE DEL POPOLO* [1868-1905]. Microfilm. San Francisco: R & E Research Associates, 1970. [The first Italian Newspaper in California].

707. "L'emigrazione italiana e la California," *L'Italia coloniale,* v. 1 (April-May, 1903), pp. 420-440.

708. MICHELI, GIUSEPPE, "I lavoratori italiani nel West Virginia." *Italia Coloniale* (1903).

709. PENATTONI, GIVACCHINO V. *Professionisti italiani e funzionari pubblici italo-americani in California.* Sacramento: Stabilimento tipografico di G.V. Penattoni, 1935.

710. PATRIZI, E. *Gli italiani in California.* San Francisco, 1911.

711. PEIXOTTO, ERNEST. "Italy in California," *Scribner's Magazine,* v. 48 (1910), pp. 75-84.

712. PERILLI, GIOVANNI. *Colorado and the Italians in Colorado. Il Colorado e gl'Italiani nel Colorado.* Denver, 1922.

713. RADIN, PAUL. *The Italians of San Francisco: their adjustment and acculturation.* California, Relief Administration. Cultural Anthropology Project. San Francisco, 1935. Reprinted, San Francisco: R & E Research Associates, 1970.

714. ROLLE, ANDREW F. 'Italy in California," *Pacific Spectator*, v. 9 (Fall 1955), pp. 408-419.

715. ROLLE, ANDREW F. "Success in the Sun: Italians in California," *The Westerners*. Los Angeles Corral. Los Angeles: Brand Book, 1961.

716. ROLLE, ANDREW F. "The Italian Moves Westward: Jesuit Missionaries formed the vanguard of Italy's many-sided impact on the frontier," *Montana* [the Magazine of Western History], Vol. 16 (January 1966), pp. 13-24.

717. RUBIERI, ERMOLAO. *Dall'Italia in California*. Firenze: Tip. Civelli, 1878.

718. SCHIAVO, GIOVANNI. "The Italian Fishermen in California," *Vigo Review* (December 1938).

719. SCHIAPPO, PIETRO L. *Nota sull'emigrazione italiana in California*. Torino: Roux, 1899.

720. SCOTT, WINFIELD. "Old wine in new bottles. When Italy comes to California through the Panama canal--what then?" *Sunset*, v. 30 (May 1913), pp. 519-526.

721. SPERONI, CHARLES. "The Development of the Columbus Day Pageant of San Francisco," *Western Folklore*, vol. 7 (1948), pp. 325-35; "California Fisherman's Festivals," *Ibid.*, vol. 14 (1955), pp. 77-91.

722. VANZI, LEONETO. "Una grave minaccia alla piu fiorente industria italiana in California," *Rivista Coloniale* (Marzo 1915).

D.   *Miscellanea*

723. "A friend of the Italian," *Outlook,* v. 98 (1911), pp. 565-566.

724. AARONSON, R.R.   "Farewell to Sicily," *Common Ground,* v. 8, no. 4 (Summer 1948), pp. 11-19.

725. ADAMIC, LOUIS.   "The plight of an 'Italian' boy," pp. 149-155, *Two-Way Passage.* New York: Harper, 1941.

726. ADAMIC, LOUIS.   "Americans from Italy," pp. 19-36, *A Nation of Nations.* New York: Harper, 1944.

727. "Aliens?" *Nation,* v. 118 (June 25, 1924), pp. 725-726.

728. American Italian Historical Association. *Newsletter* (1966-   ) and *miscellanea.*

729. ANDERSON, NELS.   *The social antecedents of a slum: A developmental study of the East Harlem area.* (Unpublished doctoral thesis, New York University, 1930).

730. ASCOLI, MAX.   "No. 38 Becomes a Citizen," *Atlantic Monthly,* Vol. CLXV (February, 1940), pp. 168-174.

731. ASCOLI, MAX.   "On the Italian Americans," *Common·Ground,* Vol. 3 (1942), pp. 45-49.

732. ASCOLI, MAX.   "The Italian American," R.M. MacIver, ed. *Group relations and group antagonisms.* New York: Harper, 1944.

733. BANFIELD, EDWARD C.   *The Moral Basis of a Backward Society,* New York: Free Press, 1958. [On Southern Italian society.]

734. "Beams thrown from Garibaldi's candles," *Survey,* v. 38 (June 30, 1917), pp. 293-294.

735. BEEDE, VINCENT VAN MARTER.   "Italians in America," *Chautauquan,* v. 34, (January 1902), pp. 422-424.

736. BERTI, LUIGI.   "Italiani in America," *Civiltà fascista* (1937), pp. 444-453.

737. BIDDLE, FRANCIS BEVERLEY.   *Americans of Italian origin: an address by the Honorable Francis Biddle delivered at the Columbus Day celebration, Carnegie Hall, New York.* ...Monday, October 12, 1942. [Broadcast over a nationwide hookup of the Mutual broadcasting system.] New York, 1942.

738. BONI, ANTONIO. *Di alcuni stati dell'America.* Vincenza: 1910.

739. BOURNE, RANDOLPH. "Emerald Lake," *New Republic,* v. 9 (January 6, 1917), 267-268. [Italian Colony]

740. BREMNER, R.H. "Children with the organ man," *American Quarterly,* Vol. 8 (Fall 1956), pp. 277-282. [Child Labor]

741. BROWN, MABEL A. "Aliens à la mode," *Christian Century,* v. 47 (October 15, 1930), pp. 1247-1249.

742. BROWN, FRANCIS J. "Italian Americans," pp. 257-270. F. Brown and J. Roucek, eds. *One America. The history, contributions and present problems of our racial and national minorities.* New York: Prentice-Hall, 1945.

743. BRUZZOLESI, VITTORIO. *Gli americani italiani e la guerra.* Milano: Alfieri & Lacroix, 1919.

744. CAHNMAN, W.J. "The Italians in America," *Jewish Frontier,* (February, 1946), pp. 8-10.

745. CALITRI, ANTONIO. *Canti del Nord-America.* Roma: Alberto Stock, 1925.

746. CAPPONI, GUIDO. *Italy and Italian in early American periodicals, (1741-1830).* Unpublished doctoral thesis, University of Wisconsin, 1958.

747. CARNOVALE, LUIGI. *Il giornalismo degli emigrati italiani nel Nord America.* Chicago: Casa editrice del giornale "L'Italia," 1909.

748. CARR, JOHN FOSTER. "The Italian in the United States," *World's Work.* v. 8 (1904), pp. 5393-5404.

749. CARR, JOHN FOSTER. "The coming of the Italian," *Outlook,* v. 82 (February 29, 1906), pp. 419-431.

750. CARR, JOHN FOSTER. *The Coming of the Italian.* New York: The Liberal Immigration League, 1906.

751. CARR, JOHN FOSTER. *Immigrant and Library: Italian Helps.* New York: The Immigrant Education League, 1914. [Intended as a guide for librarians wishing to provide materials for Italian immigrants. Lists of works in Italian and English.]

752. CARR, JOSEPH FOSTER. "L'americanizzazione degli italiani," *Il Carroccio,* v. 1 (May 1915), pp. 8-9.

753. CARR, JOHN FOSTER. *War's End: the Italian Immigrant Speaks of the Future.* New York: The Immigrant Publication Soc., Inc., 1918. [Supposed discussion among a group of Italian immigrants as to what World War I will mean to their future.]

754. CARR, JOHN FOSTER. "The coming of the Italian," pp. 141-154. Philip Davis. *Immigration and Americanization.* Boston: Ginn, 1920.

755. CARTER, HUGH and BERNICE DOSTER. "Residence and occupation of naturalized Americans from Italy," *Monthly Review [Department of Justice, Immigration and Naturalization Service],* v. 9 (July 1951), pp. 5-10.

756. CASSOM, HERBERT N. "The Italians in America," *Munsey's Magazine,* v. 36 (October 1906), pp. 122-126.

757. CIANFARRA, CAMILLO. *Dell'unica protezione possibile nel Nord America.* Roma: Unione Tipografica Cooperative, 1900.

758. CIMILLUCA, SALVATORE. *The Natural History of East Harlem from 1880-to the Present.* (Unpublished M.A. thesis, New York University, 1931). [Important history of Italian community.]

759. *Circolo italiano di Boston. A cura degli Italiani di Boston.* Boston, 1906.

760. "Colonizzazione italiana negli Stati Uniti." *Italia Coloniale* (Agosto - Novembre 1904).

761. "Condizioni di inferiorità degli stranieri in America," *Bollettino dell'Emigrazione* (1912).

762. *Congresso degli Italiani negli Stati Uniti sotto gli auspici dell'Instituto Coloniale Italiano. Ordini del giorno e raccomandazioni votate.* Philadelphia: Tipografia La Voce del Popolo, 1911.

763. "Congresso degli Italiani negli Stati Uniti. Buffalo, N.Y.: 18-22 Giugno, 1912," *Rivista Coloniale* (Luglio 1912).

764. CORRESCA, ROCCO. "The biography of a bootblack," *Independent,* v. 54 (December 4, 1902), pp. 2863-2867.

765. CORSI, EDWARD. "The voice of the Immigrant." *Outlook,* vol. LXVII (September 21, 1927), pp. 88-90.

766. CORSI, EDWARD. "Italian Americans and their children," *Annals, American Academy of Political and Social Science,* (September 1942), pp. 100-106.

767. CORSI, EDWARD. "Our Italian fellow-Americans," *American Mercury,* v. 55 (August 1942), pp. 197-205.

768. *COVELLO PAPERS.* [East Harlem, New York City Italian Community] A rich collection of reports, papers, correspondence and memorabilia collected by Leonard Covello (1887-) on the life of the largest Italian community in America [c. 1915-1945]. In possession of F. Cordasco.

769. COVELLO, LEONARD. "Italian Americans." Francis J. Brown and Joseph S. Roucek, eds. *Our racial and national minorities. Their history, contributions, and present problems.* New York: Prentice Hall, 1937.

770. COVELLO, LEONARD. *The Italians in America.* New York: Casa Italiana Education Bureau. Bulletin No. 6 [1932?]

771. CROCETTI, MARY C. "Italian settlers," *The Interpreter,* v. 3 (August 1924), pp. 4-7.

772. CURINGA, NICÒLA. *An italian tragedy. The Story of a humble people.* New York: Liverright, 1945.

773. DAVID-DUBOIS, RACHEL, ed. *Some of the contributions of Italy and her sons to civilization and American life.* New York: Casa Italiana Educational Bureau, Bulletin No. 3 [1935?]

774. D'AGOSTINO, PATSY. "I found $5,000,000 in a pushcart," *American Magazine,* v. 154 (September 1952), pp. 15, 107-111.

775. DAVENPORT, WILLIAM E. "The Italian immigrant in American," *Outlook,* v. 73 (January 3, 1903), pp. 29-37.

776. DE CAPITE, M. "War Comes to Little Italy," *Common Ground,* Vol. 2, No. 3 (1962), pp. 50-52.

777. DeRITIIS, B. "Italians in America," *Living Age,* v. 323 (November 22, 1924), pp. 423-426.

778. DeBIASI, M. *La Battaglia Dell'Italia negli Stati Uniti.* New York: Carroccio Publishing Company, 1927.

779. DiDOMENICA A. "Conditions among Italians in America," *Missionary Review,* v. 58 (February, 1935), pp. 71-73.

780. DiGIOVANNI, NORMAN THOMAS. "Tenements and Cadillacs...," *Nation,* v. 187 (December 13, 1958), pp. 443-445.

781. DiMARIO, M. "Little Italys," *Common Ground,* v. 2 (1942), pp. 19-27.

782. DRAKE, WILLIAM. "Pioneers next door," *The American Magazine,* v. 147 (April, 1949), pp. 21, 134-137.

783. DURLAND, KELLOGG. "Immigrants on the land. Italian colonists," *Chautauquan,* v. 50 (1908), pp. 89-90.

784. FAIRMAN, CHARLES E. "Our debt to Italy," *Congressional Record*, January 28, 1925, pp. 2606-2608.

785. FANTE, JOHN. "The Odyssey of a wop," *American Mercury*, v. 30 (September 1933), pp. 89-97.

786. FICCARA, BERNARD JOSEPH. *Zappatori* [The ditch diggers], Boston: Christopher Publishing House, 1953.

787. FORD, SEWELL. "The making of a citizen," *Harper's Weekly*, v. 51 (1907), pp. 1764-1765.

788. FRANKLIN, LAWRENCE. "The Italian in America: what he has been, what he shall be," *Catholic World*, v. 71 (April, 1900), pp. 67-80.

789. GARLICK, RICHARD., ed. *Italy and the Italians in Washington's time.* [Contributions by Angelo Flavio Guidi, Giuseppe Prezzolini, Bruno Roselli, Luigi Russo]. New York: Italian Publishers, 1933.

790. GATTI, ATTILIO. "It can't happen anywhere but here," *Saturday Evening Post*, v. 216 (September 18, 1943), pp. 37, 72.

791. GEDDES, JAMES JR. "Italian contribution to America," *Current Affairs* [Boston Chambers of Commerce] July 15, 1913.

792. GLANZ, RUDOLF. *Jew and Italian: Historic group relations and the New Immigration, 1881-1924.* New York: Ktav Publishing Co., 1971.

793. *Gli italiani negli Stati Uniti d'America.* New York: Italian American Directory Company, 1909.

794. GOGGIO, EMILIO. "Italians in American History." *The Italian Historical Society* [New York] 1930.

795. GROSE, HOWARD B. *Aliens or Americans?* New York: Eaton & Maine, 1906 (c. by the Young People's Missionary Movement).

796. GROSSI, VINCENZO. *Questioni di geografia coloniale. Gli Italiani negli Stati Uniti (A proposito di un recente successo diplomatico dell'on. Blanc).* Palermo: Sandron, 1895.

797. "Italian population of the United States," *Chautauquan*, v. 35, no. 3 (June 1902), p. 219.

798. *Italian culture and the Western Tradition. Some aspects of Italy's contribution to Western life and culture as presented at the conference sponsored by the Italian department of Columbia University.* Casa Italiana of Columbia University, Saturday, April 7, 1951. New York: S.F. Vanni.

799. *Italian culture in the twentieth century. Some aspects of Italy's contribution to Western life and culture as presented at the conference sponsored by the Italian department of Columbia University.* Held at Casa Italiana of Columbia University, April 19, 1952. New York: S. F. Vanni.

800. "Italian family in America: La Falces," *Life,* v. 35 (October 5, 1953), pp. 134-150. Comments: v. 35 (October 26, 1953), pp. 12, 15-16.

801. "Italiani in alcuni Stati dell'America del Nord," *Bollettino dell'Emigrazione* (1902).

802. "Italians in America," *Putnam's Magazine,* v. 9 (January 1857), pp. 1-8.

803. "Italians in the United States," *Review of Reviews,* v. 21, no. 1 (January, 1900), p. 84.

804. "Italians in America," *Catholic World,* v. 120 (January 1925), pp. 541-542.

805. "Italians in the United States," *Literary Digest,* v. 93 (April 23, 1927), pp. 30-31.

806. "Italy in America," *Independent,* v. 70, no. 3246 (February 16, 1911), pp. 370-371.

807. "Italy Rejects our deportees," *America,* vol. 88 (January 17, 1953), 414-415.

808. "Italy's sons in America. T.A. Daly's dialect ballads," *Literary Digest,* v. 93 (April 23, 1927), pp. 81-83.

809. JENKINS, HESTER.   "And we have been calling them 'Dagoes'," *World Outlook,* v. 3 (October 1907), p. 61.

810. JONES, MORRIS J.   "The Italians," pp. 78-81. *Americans all, immigrants all.* Washington: Federal Radio Education Committee, 1939.

811. KELLY, MARY.   "The Work of the Italian Auxiliary," *La Voce dell'Emigrato.* Vol. 8 (February - March, 1931), p. 35.

812. KELLY, MARY.   "Italian Immigrants as They Really are," *La Voce dell'Emigrato,* vol. 4 (October - November, 1927), pp. 13-14.

813. LATHROP, M.D.   "Zia Gracia," *Common Ground,* Vol. 1. No. 4 (1941), pp. 18-23.

814. "Lay Off The Italians," *Collier's,* Vol. 106. (August 3, 1940), p. 54.

815. LeCONTE, RENÉ.   *Les Italiens dans l'Amerique du Nord. Etude sur l'emigration italienne.* [Thèse pour le doctorat. Université de Paris, Faculté de droit] Paris: Libr. des Facultes, A.Michelon, 1908.

816. LERDA, GIOVANNI. "Gli italiani all'estero," *Rivista italiana di sociologia* (1899), pp. 619-631.

817. "Little Italy in war-time," *Literary Digest,* v. 50 (June 12, 1915), pp. 1409-1414.

818. MAISEL, ALBERT Q. "Italians among us," *Readers Digest,* v. 66 (January 1955), p. 1-6.

819. MAISEL, ALBERT Q. "The Italians," *They all Chose America.* New York: Thomas Nelson, 1955.

820. MACCHIORO, GINO. "Il nostro avvenire in America," *Nuova Antologia,* v. 84 (December 1, 1899), pp. 522-538; v. 85 (January 16, 1900), pp. 262-273.

821. MANGANO, ANTONIO. "What America did for Leonardo," *World Outlook,* v. 3 (October, 1917), p. 10.

822. MARINONI, ANTONIO. *Come ho 'fatto' l'America.* Milano: Edizioni Athena, 1932.

823. MARINI, BRUNO. *Primo: Non aver fame.* Rocca San Casciano: Capelli, 1958.

824. MARRARO, HOWARD R. "Eleuterio Felice Foresti," *Columbia University Quarterly* (March 1933), pp. 34-64.

825. MARRARO, HOWARD. *Relazioni fra l'Italia e gli Stati Uniti.* Roma: Edizioni dell'Ateneo, 1954.

826. MARRARO, HOWARD R. *Phillip Mazzei, Virginia's agent in Europe.* The story of his mission as related in his own dispatches and other documents. [Unpublished manuscript in the New York Public Library.]

827. MARINACCI, BARBARA. *They Came From Italy: The Story of Famous Italians-Americans.* New York: Dodd, 1967. [Text for Grades 8 and up.]

828. McCLELLAND, W. "Libel on Italians in the States," *Month,* Vol. 164 (September, 1934), pp. 261-264.

829. McNULTY, J. "It was Grand to be an Italian," *Illustrated Holiday,* Vol. 16 (August 1954), pp. 22-23.

830. MONACADA, F. "Little Italy of 1850," *Atlantica Magazine,* January 1933.

831. MONDELLO, SALVATORE. "The Magazine *Charities* and the Italian Immigrants, 1903-14," *Journalism Quarterly,* vol. 44 (Spring 1967), pp. 91-98.

832. NELLI, HUMBERT S. *The Role of the "Colonial" press in the Italian-American Community of Chicago 1886-1921.* Unpublished doctoral thesis, University of Chicago, 1965.

833. ODENCRANTZ, LOUISE. "Why Jennie hates flowers," *World Outlook,* v. 3 (October 1917), pp. 12-13.

834. "Operai Italiani negli Stati Uniti," *Bollettino dell'Emigrazione* (1908).

835. ORSINI, RATTO MARIO. *L'avvenire degli italo-americani.* Milano: Fratelli Treves, 1933.

836. "Our Italian immigrants." *Outlook,* v. 76 (April 16, 1904), pp. 911-912.

837. "Our Italian immigration," *Nation,* v. 80 (April 20, 1905), p. 304.

838. PAGANO, JO. "Awinding We Did Go," *Atlantic Monthly,* Vol. CLIX, (June 1937), pp. 743-54. [Italian-American family life.]

839. PARK, ROBERT E. and HERBERT A. MILLER. "The Italians;" "The Italian community," *Old world traits transplanted.* New York: Harper, 1921.

840. PECORINI, ALBERTO. "Our Italian problem," *Review of Reviews,* v. 43 (1911), pp. 236-237.

841. PECORINI, ALBERTO. "The Italians in the United States," *The Forum,* v. 45 (January 1911), pp. 15-29.

842. PILEGGI, NICHOLAS. "How We Italians Discovered America and kept it pure while giving it lots of singers, judges, and other swell people." *Esquire,* Vol. 69. (June 1968), pp. 80-82.

843. PILEGGI, NICHOLAS. "The Risorgimento of Italian power: The red, white and greening of New York," *New York,* vol. 4 (June 7, 1971), pp. 26-36.

844. PREZZOLINI, GIUSEPPE. *America con gli stivali.* Firenze: Valecchi, 1950.

845. PUZO, MARIO. "The Italians, American style," *New York Times Magazine* (August 6, 1967).

846. RICCI, VITTORIO ROLANDI. *Italy-America Society: Address* delivered by his Excellency the Royal Italian Ambassador, Senator Vittorio Rolandi Ricci. Hotel Astor. Thursday evening, April 14th, 1921. New York, 1921.

847. ROBERTS, KENNETH L. "Guests from Italy," *Saturday Evening Post,* v. 193 (August 21, 1920), pp. 10-11, 130-143.

848. ROBBINS, JANE E. "Italians today, Americans tomorrow," *Outlook*, v. 80 (June 10, 1905), pp.382-384.

849. ROSELLI, BRUNO. *Colonel Francis Vigo--savior of the Midwest.* [1932?]

850. ROSELLI, BRUNO. *Vigo: A forgotten builder of the American republic.* Boston: The Stratford Co., 1933.

851. ROSELLI, BRUNO. *How shall we honor Vigo?* An address in response to the award of the honorary degree of Doctor of Literature by Vincennes University, June 5, 1936.

852. ROSSI, A. "Per la tutela degli italiani negli Stati Uniti," *Bollettino dell'emigrazione*, 1904.

853. ROSSO, AUGUSTO. "The United States and Italy," *Italy America Monthly*, v. 2 (February 25, 1935), pp. 1-7.

854. ROSS, EDWARD A. "Italians in America," *Century*, v. 88 (July 1914), pp. 439-445.

855. RUBIN, VERA D. *Fifty years in Rootville. A study in the dynamics of acculturation of an Italian immigrant group in an urban community.* New York, 1951.

856. RUOTOLO, O. "Americans First," *Magazine of Art*, Vol. 30. (August 1937), p. 466.

857. SCALIA, EUGEN S. "Frederico Confalonieri in America," *Italy-America Monthly*, v. 1 (March 15, 1934), pp. 10-13; (April 15, 1934), pp. 12-15.

858. SCANLAND, J.J. "Italian quarter mosaic," *Overland Monthly*, n.s. v. 47 (1906), pp. 327-334.

859. SCHERMERHORN, RICHARD A. "The Italo-American: the latest arrival." *These our people. Minorities in American cultures.* Boston: D.C. Heath, 1949.

860. SCHULTZE, E. "Die Italiener in den Vereinigten Staaten," *Zeitschrift für Sozialwissenschaft*, 9 Jahrg. (October 1906), pp. 624-666.

861. SCUDDER, VIDA. "Denison house and the Italians," *Commons* (May 1905).

862. SEXTON, PATRICIA. *Spanish Harlem.* New York: Harper & Row, 1965. [Italian community.] See also, F. Cordasco, "Spanish Harlem: The Anatomy of Poverty," *Phylon: The Atlanta Review of Race & Culture*, vol. 26 (Summer 1965), pp. 195-196.

863. SFORZA, CARLO. *The real Italians.* New York: Columbia University Press, 1942.

864. SEABROOK, WILLIAM A. "Italian Americans." *These foreigners.* New York: Harcourt Brace, 1938.

865. SEABROOK, WILLIAM A. "Americans first," *American Magazine,* v. 123 (June 14, 1937), pp. 14-15; 97-109. [Reply by Onorio Ruotolo in *Magazine of Art,* v. 30 (August, 1937), pp. 466; 520]

866. SPADONI, ADRIANA. "Americanizing Paolo," *Outlook,* v. 104 (August 23, 1913), pp. 920-026.

867. SPERANZA, G.L. "Italians in the United States," *Chautauquan,* Vol. 9 (1891), p. 346.

868. SPERANZA, GINO C. "A mission of peace," *Outlook,* v. 78 (September 10, 1904), pp. 128-131.

869. SPERANZA, GINO. "Handicaps in America," *Survey,* (January 1, 1910), pp. 465-472.

870. SPERANZA, GINO C. "Heart's allegiance," *Outlook,* v. 119 (May 15, 1918), p. 105.

871. SPERANZA, GINO. *Race or Nationality: A Conflict of Divided Loyalities.* Indianapolis. [1920?]

872. STEVENSON, FREDERICK B. "Italian colonies in the United States," *Public Opinion,* v. 39 (October 7, 1905), pp. 453-456.

873. SWEET, M. McD. "Italians and the public library," *Library Journal,* v. 49 (November 5, 1924), pp. 977-981.

874. SWEET, M. McD. *The Italian immigrant and his reading.* Chicago: American Library Association, 1925.

875. SWEET, M. McD. *Italian books for American libraries.* A supplement to *The Italian immigrant and his reading.* Chicago: American Library Association, 1932.

876. "The Italian Problem," *The Extension,* Volume XII (September 1917), p. 3.

877. "The Italian future in America," *Review of Reviews,* v. 21 (1900), pp. 486-487.

878. TIGANI, JOSEPH A. *Historical Reappraisal of early Italian settlers, in America.* Rowayton, Conn.: 1966.

879. TURANO, ANTHONY M.   "An immigrant father," *American Mercury*, v. 27 (October 1932), pp. 221-229.

880. UNDERHILL, RUTH M.   "Imported homes," *World Outlook*, v. 3 (October, 1917), pp. 7-8.

881. VARNEY, HAROLD L.   "The Italians in contemporary America," *Italian Historical Society*, (1932?), pp. 1-33.

882. VELIKONJA, JOSEPH.   "The Italian born in the United States, 1950," *Annals of the Association of American Geographers*, Vol. 51 (December, 1961), p. 426.

883. VELIKONJA, JOSEPH.   "Distribuzione geografica degli italiani negli Stati Uniti," *Atti. XVII Congresso Geografico Italiano* [Trieste] 1961, vol. 2, pp. 243-262.

884. VERGOTTINI, MARIO DE.   "A study of the demography of Italians abroad," *Annali di Statistica* (Roma), v. 6 (1940), pp. 47-296.

885. VILLARI, L.   "Italo-Americans today: pride in the Homeland." *World Review*, Vol. 4 (February 1938), pp. 54-56.

886. WEYL, WALTER E.   "The Italian who lived on twenty-six cents a day," *Outlook*, v. 94 (December 25, 1909), pp. 966-975.

887. "Who's Untouchable? UNICO's Protest," *America*, Vol. 103 (August 20, 1960), p. 547.

888. WITTKE, CARL F.   "The Italians." *We who built America. The saga of the immigrant.* New York: Prentice Hall, 1939.

889. "Work among Italian immigrants," *Charities*, v. 10 (February 7, 1903), pp. 122-124.

890. WRIGHT, FREDERICK H.   "How to reach Italians in America? Shall they be segregated, 'missioned', neglected or welcomed?" *Missionary Review of the World*, v. 40 (August, 1917), pp. 588-594.

891. YOUNG, STARK.   "Little dream," *New Republic*, v. 60 (November 13, 1929), pp. 353-354. [Italian community]

IV. THE SOCIOLOGY OF ITALIAN AMERICAN LIFE

A. *Social Structure: Conflict and Acculturation*
B. *Education [With Some Notices of Italian Language Instruction]*
C. *Health and Related Concerns*
D. *Religion and Missionary Work*
E. *Crime, Delinquency and Social Deviance*

UNKNOWN PHOTOGRAPHER/BOYS SITTING IN MULBERRY STREET, c. 1897/THE BETTMANN ARCHIVE

Major attention is given in this section to social structure (conflict and acculturation), and the multifaceted aspects of life in the Italian community. The controversy over whether the life styles of the Italian interstitial community were fashioned in the American cities, or were traits and social structures transplanted with little change from Italy may be explored in the antithetic views of Nelli and Vecoli (see entries *infra*); the literature seems to support Vecoli's contention that the life of the Italian subcommunity essentially reflected both the *ethos* and structure of the Italian *Mezzogiorno*. In the division on education some notices have been made of Italian language instruction, but as Professor Fucilla observed in his review of the Velikonja bibliography, "...we see no really intimate relationship between Italian in so far as it primarily concerns Italo-Americans and Italian as taught in our public schools."* The vast literature on the Sacco-Vanzetti case is only alluded to in a few titles, and reference should be made to the important study by Francis Russell, *Tragedy in Dedham* (1962); similarly, only a skeletal framework of titles on crime and the *Mafia* has been attempted: and the area of a "delinquent subculture" remains to be studied in the model furnished by Albert Cohen (*Delinquent Boys*. New York: Free Press, 1955). The titles on health and related concerns point up the neglect in this important area; and the division on religion and missionary work, despite the multiplicity on titles, is a facet of the Italian American experience which is only beginning to receive the serious attention it merits *(e.g., articles by Tomasi and Vecoli infra)*.

A.   *Social Structure: Conflict and Acculturation*

892.   ALISSI, ALBERT S.   *Boys born in little Italy: A comparison of their individual value orientations, family patterns, and peer associations.* Unpublished doctoral thesis, Western Reserve University, 1967.

893.   "Assimilating the Adult Immigrant," *Outlook*, Vol. 88 (February 1, 1908), pp. 244-245.

894.   BERTOCCI, ANGELO P.   "Memoir of my mother," *Harper's Magazine*, v. 175 (June 1937), pp. 8-10.

895.   BRANDT, LILIAN.   "A transplanted birthright. The development of the second generation of the Italian in an American environment," *Charities*, v. 12 (May 7, 1904), pp. 494-499; also, *The Charity Organization Society, 1882-1907* (New York: United Charities, 1907).

896.   BUGELSKI, B.R.   "Assimilation through intermarriage," *Social Forces*, v. 40 (December 1961), pp. 148-153.

Italica, vol. 41 (June 1964), p. 215.

897. CAMPISI, PAUL J.   *The adjustment of Italian-Americans to the war crisis.* Unpublished M.A. thesis, University of Chicago, 1942.

898. CAMPISI, PAUL J.   *A scale for the measurement of acculturation.* Unpublished doctoral thesis, University of Chicago, 1947.

899. CAMPISI, PAUL J.   "Ethnic family patterns: the Italian family in the United States," *American Journal of Sociology,* v. 53 (May 1948), pp. 443-449. Also published as, "The Italian family in the United States," Milton L. Barron, *American Minorities.* New York: Alfred Knopf, 1957.

900. CARTER, HUGH and BERNICE DOSTER.   "Social characteristics of naturalized Americans from Italy," *Monthly Review, Department of Justice, Immigration and Naturalization Service,* vol. 8 (May 1951), pp. 145-152.

901. Casa Italiana Educational Bureau. *Bulletins.* (1) 11th Annual Report, 1931-1932, Italian Teachers' Association; (2) Peter M. Riccio, Why English Speaking People Should Study Italian; (3) Rachel Davis-Dubois, ed., Some of the Contributions of Italy and her Sons to Civilization and American Life; (4) Leonard Covello, The Casa Italiana Educational Bureau – Its Purpose and Program; (5) Henry G. Doyle, The Importance of the Study of the Italian Language; (6) Leonard Covello, The Italians in America, With Maps and Research Outlines; (7) William B. Shedd, The Italian Population in New York City with Maps and Tables; (8) John J. D'Alesandre, Occupational Trends of Italians in New York City. [c. 1932-1942].

902. CAUTELA, GIUSEPPE.   "Italian funeral," *American Mercury,* v. 15 (October 1928), pp. 200-206.

903. CHILD, IRVIN LONG.   *Italian or American? The second generation in conflict.* New Haven: Published for the Institute of Human Relations by Yale University Press, 1943. Reissued with an introduction by F. Cordasco, New York: Russell & Russell, 1970 [originally, Ph.D. dissertation, Yale University, 1939].

904. COLAJANNI, NAPOLEONE.   *Razze inferiore e razze superiori o Latini e Anglosassoni.* Roma: Presso la Rivista Popolare, 1906.

905. DOUGLAS, DAVID W.   *Influence of the Southern Italian in American Society.* (Columbia University Studies in Sociology), New York: Columbia University, 1915.

906. EFRON, DAVID.   *Gesture and environment; a tentative study of some of the spatio-temporal and linguistic aspects of the gestural behavior of eastern Jews and southern Italians in New York City, living under similar as well as different environmental conditions.* Unpublished doctoral thesis, Columbia University, 1942.

907. FERMI, LAURA. "Process of Americanization," *Mademoiselle*, v. 39 (September 1954), pp. 115+.

908. FERRARI, ROBERTO. "Il problema delle razze negli Stati Uniti con speciale riferimento agli Italiani," *Rivista d'Italia e d'America* (1925-1926).

909. GANS, HERBERT J. *The Urban Villagers.* New York: Free Press, 1962. [Italian-American community of Boston].

910. GLAZER, NATHAN and DANIEL P. MOYNIHAN. *Beyond the Melting Pot: The Negroes, Puerto Ricans, Jews, Italians, and Irish of New York City.* 2nd ed. Cambridge: M.I.T. Press, 1970. [The section on Italians was written by Glazer].

911. GRIECO, ROSE. "They who mourn. [Italian-American wakes]," *Commonweal,* v. 57 (March 27, 1953), pp. 628-630.

912. GRIECO, ROSE. "Wine and fig trees," *Commonweal,* v. 60 (June 4, 1954), pp. 221-223.

913. GURNEY, MARION E. "The story of a clock," *Charities,* v. 12 (1904), pp. 499-501.

914. HOWELLS, W.D. "Our Italian assimilators," *Harper's Weekly,* v. 53 (April 10, 1909), p. 28.

915. HULL, I.L. "Special problems in Italian families," *National Conference of Social Workers,* 1924, pp. 288-291.

916. IANNI, FRANCIS A. *The Acculturation of the Italo-Americans of Norristown, Pennsylvania, 1900-1950.* Unpublished doctoral thesis, Pennsylvania State College, 1952.

917. IANNI, F.A. "Residential and occupational mobility as indices of the acculturation of an ethnic group. [The Italo-American colony in Norristown, Pa.]," *Social Forces,* v. 36 (October 1957), pp. 65-72.

918. IANNI, FRANCIS A.J. "Italo-American teen-ager," *Annals, American Academy of Political and Social Science,* v. 338 (November 1961), pp. 70-78.

919. KINGSLEY, H.L. and M. CARBONE. "Attitudes of Italian-Americans toward race prejudice," *Journal of Abnormal Psychology,* Vol. 33 (October 1938), pp. 532-537.

920. LEWIS, CHARLES A. *Communication patterns of recent immigrants: a study of three nationality groups in Metropolitan Detroit.* Unpublished doctoral thesis, University of Illinois, 1932. [Italians: pp. 32-37, 73-83, 220-225].

921. LoBELLO, NINO. *A Descriptive Analysis of Two Contiguous Ethnic Groups in New York City: A Comparative Study of the German-American Community of Ridgewood, Queens, and the Italian-American Settlement of Bushwick, Brooklyn.* [Unpublished M.S. thesis, New York University, 1944.]

922. LOLLI, GIORGIO. *et. al. Alcohol in Italian culture: food and wine in relation to sobriety among Italians and Italian-Americans.* New Haven: Yale University Center of Alcohol Studies, 1958.

923. LOPREATO, JOSEPH. "Differential Assimilation Among New Haven Italians," [Unpublished paper, 1957].

924. LOPREATO, JOSEPH. *Effects of emigration on the social structure of a Calabrian town.* Unpublished doctoral thesis, Yale University, 1960.

925. MacDONALD, JOHN S. and D. LEATRICE. "Urbanization, ethnic groups and social segmentation. [The clustering of separate groups from different rural areas; examination of the process by which neighborhoods of southern Italians rose in Northern cities of the United States.]," *Social Research,* vol. 29 (Winter 1962), pp. 433-448.

926. MacDONALD, JOHN S. and D. LEATRICE. "Chain Migration, ethnic neighborhood formation and social networks," *Milbank Memorial Fund Quarterly,* Vol. 42 (January 1964), pp. 82-97 [Southern Italians in the United States].

927. MARCUSON, LEWIS R. *The Irish, The Italians and the Jews: A Study of Three Nationality Groups as Portrayed in American Drama Between 1920 and 1960.* Unpublished doctoral thesis. University of Denver, 1966.

928. NELLI, HUMBERT S. "Italians in Urban America: A study in Ethnic Adjustment," *International Migration Review,* Vol. I. New Series (Summer 1967), pp. 38-55. [See entries for R.J. Vecoli for different view.]

929. PALISI, B.J. "Ethnic generation and family structure," *Journal of Marriage and Family,* Vol. 28 (February 1966), pp. 49-50.

930. PALISI, B.J. "Patterns of social participation in a two-generation sample of Italian-Americans," *Sociological Quarterly,* vol. 7 (Spring 1966), pp. 107-178.

931. PALISI, B.J. Ethnic Patterns of Friendship, *Phylon,* Vol. 27 (Fall 1966), pp. 217-225.

932. POMEROY, SARAH G. *The Italian.* New York: Fleming H. Revell Co., 1915.

80

933. PSATHAS, GEORGE. "Ethnicity, social class, and adolescent independence from parental control." *American Sociological Review,* vol. 22 (August 1957), pp. 415-423. [A study of Southern Italian and Eastern European Jewish ethnic group in New Haven].

934. "Religion of lucky pieces, witches and the evil eye," *World Outlook,* v. 3 (October 1917), pp. 24-25.

935. ROSELLI, BRUNO. "Our Italian immigrants: their racial backgrounds." H.P. Fairchild, ed., *Immigrant backgrounds.* New York: J. Wiley, 1927.

936. ROUCEK, JOSEPH S. "Social attitudes of native-born children of foreign-born parents," *Sociology and Social Research,* v. 22 (November 1927), pp. 149-155.

937. SEMOLINO, MARIA. *Papa's table d'hôte.* Philadelphia: Lippincott, 1952.

938. SINGER, CAROLINE. "An Italian Saturday," *Century,* v. 101, no. 5 (March 1921), pp. 590-600.

939. SPERANZA, GINO C. "How it feels to be a problem: a consideration of certain causes which prevent or retard assimilation," *Charities,* v. 12 (May 7, 1904), pp. 457-463.

940. SPERANZA, GINO C. "The Italians in congested districts," *Charities,* v. 20 (April, 1908), pp. 55-57.

941. STEINER, EDWARD A. "The Italian in America." *On the trail of the immigrant.* New York: Fleming H. Revell, 1906.

942. STRODTBECK, F.L. and OTHERS. "Evaluation of occupations: a reflection of Jewish and Italian mobility differences," *American Sociological Review,* vol. 22 (October 1957), pp. 546-553. See No. 792.

943. "The Italian problem," *Harper's Weekly,* v. 53 (July 3, 1909), p. 5.

944. "The Italian and the settlement," *Survey,* v. 30 (April 12, 1913), pp. 58-60.

945. WELD, RALPH F. "The versatile Italians," *Brooklyn is America.* New York: Columbia University Press, 1950.

946. WHEELER, THOMAS C. *The Immigrant Experience: The Anguish of Becoming an American.* New York: Dial, 1971. [Narrative by Mario Puzo]

947. WHYTE, WILLIAM F. "Race conflicts in the North End of Boston," *New England Quarterly* v. 12 (December 1939), pp. 623-642.

948. WHYTE, WILLIAM F. *Street corner society: the social structure of an Italian slum.* 2nd edition. Chicago: University of Chicago Press, 1955. [Revision of Ph.D. dissertation, University of Chicago, 1943]

949. WILLIAMS, PHYLLIS H. *South Italian folkways in Europe and America a handbook for social workers, visiting nurses, school teachers, and physicians.* New Haven: Published for the Institute of Human Relations by Yale University Press, 1938. Reissued with An Introductory note by F. Cordasco, New York: Russell & Russell, 1969.

950. WINSEY, VALENTINE ROSSILLI. *A Study of the Effect of Transplantation upon Attitudes toward the United States of Southern Italians in New York City as revealed by Survivors of the Mass-Migration, 1887-1915.* Unpublished doctoral dissertation, New York University, 1966.

951. ZALOHA, ANNA. *A Study of the Persistence of Italian Customs Among 143 Families of Italian Descent.* [Unpublished M.A. Thesis, Northwestern University, 1937].

B.   *Education [With Some Notices of Italian Language Instruction]*

952. ADDAMS, JANE.   "Foreign-born children in the primary grades: Italian families in Chicago," *National Education Association of the U.S. Journal of Proceedings and Addresses,* v. 36 (1897), pp. 104-112.

953. "America's interest in the education of Italian children," *Review Of Reviews,* v. 36 (1907), pp. 375-376.

954. ALTROCCHI, RUDOLPH.   "The study of Italian in retrospect and prospect," *Modern Language Journal,* v. 12 (May 1929), pp. 630-634.

955. ARSENIAN, SETH.   *Bilingualism and mental development: a study of the intelligence and the social background of bilingual children in New York City.* New York: *Teacher's College,* Columbia University, 1937.

956. AYRES, LEONARD P.   *Laggards in Our Schools.* New York: The Charities Publication Committee [of the Russell Sage Foundation]. 1909. [Useful data and information on Italian school children]

957. BEARD, ANNIE E.S.   *Our Foreign-Born Citizens,* (New York: Crowell, 1922), [Chap. on Angelo Patri: "An Italian Immigrant who Influenced public school education." pp. 266-74.]

958. BERE, MAY.   *A Comparative Study of the Mental Capacity of Children of Foreign Parentage.* New York: Columbia University, 1924. (No. 154 in Teachers College Contributions to Education.) [Compares Italian, Jewish, and "Bohemian" children.]

959. BERROL, SELMA.   "Immigrants at School: New York City, 1900-1910," *Urban Education,* vol. 4 (October 1969), pp. 220-230.

960. BOTTA, VINCENZO.   *Intorno alle scuole italiane a New York.* Milano: Daelli, 1864.

961. BRUNIALTI, ATTILIO.   "Un scuole italiane fuori d'Italia," *Nuova Antologia* (Aprile 1884).

962. BUSCEMI, PHILIP A.   "The Sicilian immigrant and his language problems," *Sociology and Social Research,* v. 12 (November - December 1927), pp. 137-143.

963. Children of Immigrants in Schools. vols. 29-33 of *Report of the Immigration Commission.* 41 vols. (Washington: Government Printing Office, 1911). Republished with *An Introductory Essay* by F. Cordasco, Metuchen, N.J.: Scarecrow Reprint Corp., 1970. [A vast repository of data on educational history of immigrant children in America. Detailed analysis of backgrounds, nativity, school progress and home environments of school children in 32 American cities.] See also, Morris I. Berger, *The Settlement, the immigrant and the public school* (unpublished doctoral thesis, Columbia University, 1956); and F. Cordasco, "Educational Pelagianism: The Schools and the Poor," *Teachers College Record,* vol. 69 (April 1968), pp. 705-09. See No. 100.

964. CINFOLETTI, MANLIO. *Le scuole parrocchiali negli Stati Uniti d'America e in particolare le italiane.* Roma: Tip. Pontificia Pio IX, 1918.

965. CORDASCO, F. "The challenge of the non-English speaking child in American schools," *School & Society* (March 30, 1968), pp. 198-201. [On the enactment of the bilingual amendments (Title VII) of the Elementary and Secondary Education Act.]

966. CORDASCO, F. "The Children of Immigrants in the Schools: Historical Analogues of Educational Deprivation," *Kansas Journal of Sociology,* vol. 6 (Fall 1970), pp. 143-152. [Italian Children in American schools.]

967. COSENZA, MARIO E. *The study of Italian in the United States.* Italy-America Society, 1924.

968. COVELLO, LEONARD. "Language usage in Italian families," *Atlantica,* (October - November 1934).

969. COVELLO, LEONARD. "A High School and its Immigrant Community," *Journal of Educational Sociology,* vol. 9 (February 1936), pp. 333-346. [Benjamin Franklin High School, East Harlem.]

970. COVELLO, LEONARD. The Casa Italiana Educational Bureau--Its purpose and aim. New York: *The Casa Italiana Educational Bureau, Bulletin,* No. 4 [c. 1942]

971. COVELLO, LEONARD. *The social background of the Italo-American school child. A study of the Southern Italian family mores and their effect on the school situation in Italy and America.* Edited and with an introduction by F. Cordasco. Leiden, The Netherlands: E.J. Brill, 1967. [Revision of doctoral thesis, New York University, 1944.]

972. CONCESTRÉ, MARIE J.   *Adult education in a local area: A study of a decade in the life and education of the adult immigrant in East Harlem, New York City*. Unpublished doctoral thesis. New York University, 1944. [A major study of the Italian community].

973. FISHMAN, JOSHUA A.   *Language loyalty in the United States. The maintenance and perpetuation of non-English mother tongues by American ethnic and religious groups*. The Hague: Mouton, 1966. [Important work on language retention by Italian Americans.]

974. GARDINI, GIOVANNI and W.T. ROTT.   "A Comparison of the Detroit first-grade tests given in Italian and English," *Psychological Clinic,* v. 15 (May - June 1923), pp. 101-108.

975. GISOLFI, ANTHONY M.   "Italo-American: what he has borrowed from American English and what he is contributing to the American language," *Commonweal,* v. 30 (July 21, 1939), pp. 311-313.

976. GOLDEN, HERBERT H.   "The teaching of Italian: the 1962 Balance Sheet," *Italica,* vol. 39 (1962), pp. 275-288. [A significant statement on the decline in Italian language instruction in the U.S.] See No. 991.

977. GRANDGENT, C.H.   "Dante in the United States," *Italy-America Review,* v. 2 (Winter, 1937), pp. 1-4.

978. HUTCHINSON, E.P.   *Immigrants and their Children, 1850-1950*. New York: John Wiley and Sons, 1956.

979. MARRARO, H.R.   "Da Ponte and Foresti: The Introduction of Italian at Columbia University," *Columbia University Quarterly* (March 1937).

980. MARRARO, HOWARD R.   "The teaching of Italian in America in the eighteenth century." *Modern Language Journal,* v. 25 (1941), pp. 120-125.

981. MARRARO, HOWARD R.   "Pioneer Italian teachers of Italian in the United States," *Modern Language Journal,* v. 28 (November 1944), pp. 555-582.

982. MARRARO, HOWARD R.   "Doctoral dissertations in Italian accepted by Romance language departments in American universities 1876-1950" *Bulletin of Bibliography,* v. 20 (January - April, 1951), pp. 94-99.

983. MATTHEWS, SISTER MARY FABIAN.   *The Role of the Public School in the Assimilation of the Italian Immigrant Child in New York City 1900-1914*. Unpublished doctoral thesis, Fordham University, 1966. [Should be used in conjunction with Covello, No. 971.]

984. MAY, ELLEN   "Italian education and immigration," *Education,* v. 28 (March, 1908), pp. 450-453.

985. MEAD, MARGARET. "Group intelligence tests and linguistic disability among Italian children," *School & Society*, v. 25 (April 16, 1927), pp. 465-468.

986. MOORE, SARAH WOOL. "The Teaching of Foreigners." *The Survey*, vol. XXIV (June 4, 1910), pp. 386-392.

987. MOORHEAD, ELIZABETH. "A school for Italian laborers," *Outlook*, v. 88 (February 29, 1908), pp. 499-504.

988. PATRI, ANGELO. *A school master in the great city.* New York: Macmillan, 1917. See also No. 957.

989. PREZZOLINI, GIUSEPPE. "An Italian surveys the American University." New York: Casa Italiana, Education Department. [c. 1942]

990. ROSELLI, BRUNO. *The teaching of Italian in the United States: an historical survey.* New York: J.J. Little & Ives, 1934.

991. ROSELLI, BRUNO. *Italian yesterday and today: a history of Italian teaching in the United States.* Boston: The Stratford Co., 1935.

992. ROSSI, PETER H. and ALICE S. ROSSI. "Parochial School Education in America." *Daedalus*, vol. 90 (Spring 1961), pp. 300-328. [Observations concerning Italian attendance in Catholic parochial schools.]

993. "Schools for Immigrant Laborers," *The Outlook*, vol. XLII (August 7, 1909), pp. 823-24.

994. "Scuole Italiane all'Estero," *Bollettino del Ministero degli Affari Esteri* (1902-1926).

995. SEAGO, D.W. and T.S. KOLDIN. "Comparative study of the mental capacity of sixth grade Jewish and Italian children," *School & Society*, v. 22 (October 31, 1925), pp. 564-568.

996. SEROTA, KATHRYN E. "A comparative study of 100 Italian children at the six-year level," *Psychological Clinic*, v. 16 (October 1927), pp. 216-231.

997. SIMONCINI, FORREST. "The San Francisco Italian dialect: a study," *Orbis* [Louvain]. v. 8 (1959), pp. 342-354.

998. SMITH, TIMOTHY L. "Immigrant Social aspirations and American education, 1880-1930," *American Quarterly*, vol. 21 (Fall 1969), pp. 523-43.

999. SPADONI, ADRIANA. "The lesson," *Outlook*, v. 104 (June 20, 1913), pp. 443-449.

1000. TAIT, JOSEPH W. *Some Aspects of the Effect of the Dominant American Culture Upon Children of Italian-Born Parents*. New York: Columbia University, 1942. (Teachers College Contributions to Education). [Reprinted With A Foreword by F. Cordasco, New York: Augustus M. Kelley, 1971.]

1001. "The Italian interuniversity bureau at Columbia University," *School & Society*, v. 47 (February 26, 1938), pp. 267-268.

1002. THOMPSON, FRANK V. *Schooling of the Immigrant*. New York. Harper, 1920. See also Alan M. Thomas, "American Education and the immigrant, *Teachers College Record*, vol. 55 (1953-54), pp. 253-67; also, F. Cordasco, "Summer camp education for underprivileged children," *School & Society*, vol. 93 (Summer 1965).

1003. *TOUR OF LITTLE ITALY*. W.P.A. Education Program. Chicago Board of Education. Chicago. January 20, 1937.

1004. TURANO, ANTHONY M. "The speech of Little Italy," *American Mercury*, v. 26 (July 1932), pp. 356-359.

1005. VAUGHAN, HERBERT H. "Italian and its dialects as spoken in the United States," *American Speech*, v. 1 (April - May 1926), pp. 431-435.

1006. VINCI, ADOLFO. *La scuole e la cultura italiana negli Stati Uniti*. Roma, 1910.

1007. "Vocational training for Italian emigrants," *Interpreter Releases*, v. 4 (March 18, 1927), pp. 50-51. See S. Cohen, "The Industrial Education Movement, 1906-1917," *American Quarterly*, vol. 20 (1968), pp. 95-110.

1008. WHEATON, H.H. *Recent progress in the Education of immigrants*. Washington: Government Printing Office, 1915. See, in this connection, *Bibliography of Publications of the U.S. Office of Education 1867-1959*. With An Introductory Note by F. Cordasco. Totowa, N.J.: Rowman and Littlefield, 1971.

1009. BERNARDY, AMY.   "La tutela delle donne e dei fanciulli italiani negli Stati Uniti d'America." *Atti del II Congresso degli Italiani all'estero.* Roma: Tipografia Editrice Nazionale, 1911; also, "Sulle condizioni delle donne e dei fanciulli italiani negli Stati del centro e dell'Ovest della Confederazione del Nord America," *Bollettino del'Emigrazione* (1911).

1010. BREED, R.L.   "Italians fight tuberculosis," *Survey,* v. 23 (February 12, 1910), pp. 702-703.

1011. BREMNER, ROBERT H., ed.   *Children and Youth in America: A Documentary History.* vol. I (1600-1865); vol. II, 1866-1932: Parts 1-6; Parts 7-8. Cambridge: Harvard University Press, 1970-71.

1012. BRINDISI, ROCCO.   "The Italian and public health," *Charities,* v. 12 (May 7, 1904), pp. 483-486.

1013. CHIARAVILLO, EDVIGE.   *La protezione della donna italiana all'estro.* Torino: Tip. Barvalle, 1911.

1014. DINWIDDIE, EMILY W.   "Some aspects of Italian housing and social conditions in Philadelphia," *Charities,* v. 12 (May 1904), pp. 490-494.

1015. GEBHART, JOHN C.   *Growth and Development of Italian Children in New York.* New York: The Association for the Improvement of the Condition of the Poor, 1924.

1016. GILLETT, LUCY H.   "Factors influencing nutrition work among Italians," *Journal of Home Economics,* v. 14 (January 1922), pp. 14-19.

1017. GRIFFITH, ELOISE.   "A social worker looks at Italians," *Journal of Educational Sociology,* v. 5 (1931), pp. 172-177.

1018. GRIEL, CECILE L.   *I problemi della madre in un paese nuovo.* New York: Y.W.C.A., U.S. National Board. Division on work for foreign born women, 1919.

1019. *Istituto italiano di beneficenza e l'ospedale italiano di New York.* New York: Tip. Fabbri, 1906.

1020. McMAIN, ELEANOR.   "Behind the yellow fever in Little Palermo [Housing conditions which New Orleans should shake itself free from along the summer's scourge]," *Charities,* v. 15 (November 4, 1905), pp. 152-159.

1021. MOSELEY, DAISY H. "The Catholic social worker in an Italian district," *Catholic World,* v. 114 (February 1922), pp. 618-628.

1022. MUDGE, G.G. "Italian dietary adjustments," *Journal of Home Economics,* v. 15 (April 1923), pp. 181-185.

1023. NIZZARDINI, GENOEFFA. "Health among the Italians in New York City," *Atlantica,* v. 16 (December 1934), pp. 406-408, 411.

1024. NIZZARDINI, GENOEFFA. "Infant mortality for Manhattan, Brooklyn and Bronx, 1916-1931," *Italy-America Monthly,* v. 2 (May 25, 1935), pp. 12-17.

1025. NIZZARDINI, GENOEFFA and N.F. JOFFE. *Italian food patterns and their relationship to wartime problems of food and nutrition.* Washington, D.C.: The Committee on Food Habits, National Research Council, 1943.

1026. REED, DOROTHY. *Leisure time of girls in a "Little Italy."* A comparative study of the leisure interests of adolescent girls of foreign parentage living in a metropolitan community, to determine the presence or absence of interest differences in relation to behavior. Portland, Oregon: 1932. [Ph.D. thesis, Columbia University, 1932.]

1027. ROBERTS, MARJORIE. "Italian girls on American soil," *Mental Hygiene,* v. 13 (October 1929), pp. 757-768.

1028. ROBINSON, GILBERT K. "Catholic birth-rate: further facts and implications," *American Journal of Sociology,* v. 41 (May 1936), pp. 757-766.

1029. ROSATI, TEODORICO. "Servizi sanitari per l'emigrazione durante gli anni 1910-1915," *Annali di Medicina Navale* (1916).

1030. ROSE, ARNOLD M. "A research note on the influence of immigration on the birth rate [Italians in Chicago]," *American Journal of Sociology,* v. 47 (January 1942), pp. 614-621.

1031. SERGI, GIUSEPPE. *Il preteso mutamento delle forme fisiche nei discendenti degli immigrati in America.* Scansano: Tip. Delgi Olmi, 1912. See No. 100, *Bodily Form of descendents of immigrants. [Report of the Immigration Commission,* 1911]

1032. SPENGLER, JOSEPH J. "The fecundity of native and foreign born women in New England," *The Brookings Institute, Pamphlet Series,* v. 2 (1930). See No. 100, *Fecundity of immigrant women. [Report of the Immigration Commission, 1911]*

1033. SPICER, DOROTHY G. "Health superstitions of the Italian immigrant," *Hygeia,* v. 4 (May 1926), pp. 266-269.

1034. STELLA, ANTONIO.   *The Effects of urban congestion on Italian women and children*. New York: William Wood, 1908.

1035. STELLA, ANTONIO.   "Tuberculosis and the Italians in the United States," *Charities*, v. 12 (May 7, 1904), pp. 486-489.

1036. STELLA, ANTONIO.   "The prevalence of tuberculosis among Italians in the United States," *Transactions of the Sixth International Congress on Tuberculosis*. Washington, September 28 - October 5, 1908, v. 1-5. Philadelphia: W.F. Fell, 1908.

1037. STELLA, ANTONIO.   "[Tuberculosis] among the Italians," *Charities*, v. 21 (November 7, 1908), p. 248.

1038. STELLA, ANTONIO.   *La lotta contro la tubercolosi fra gli Italiani nella città di New York ed effetti dell'urbanesimo*. Roma: Tip. Colombo, 1912.

D. *Religion and Missionary Work*

1039. "A suburban church," *Commonweal*, v. 40 (August 11, 1944), p. 405.

1040. ABBOTT, GRACE. "Leo XIII and the Italian Catholics in the United States," *The American Ecclesiastical Review*, Vol. 1 (February 1889), pp. 41-45.

1041. *Adventures of Tony* New York: Presbyterian Board of Home Missions [c. 1912]. An illustrated tract/lecture. See No. 1100.

1042. An Old Missionary, "Priests for Italian Immigrants." *The American Ecclesiastical Review*. Vol. 20 (1899), pp. 513-516.

1043. *Apostolo degli italiani emigrati nelle Americhe, ossia Mons. Scalabrini e l'istituto dei suoi Missionari.* Piacenza: Tipografia Editrice del Maino, 1909.

1044. BANDINI, A. *Relazioni della Società Italiana di San Raffaele in New York nel primo anno della sua fondazione.* Piacenza: Tipografia Marchetti e Porta, 1892.

1045. BANDINI, ALBERT. "Concerning the Italian problem," *Ecclesiastic Review*, v. 62 (1920), pp. 278-185.

1046. BELCREDI, G. G. "Gli italiani nel Nord America (un colloquio con Monsignor Scalabrini)," *L'Italia coloniale*, vol. 1 (January 1902), pp. 33-38.

1047. BENEDICTUS PP. XV "Lettera a Mons. Tommaso Giuseppe, vescovo di Trenton, in cui vengono lodate le sue paterne cure verso gli Italiani," *Inter praeclareas laudes*, 10 Dicembre 1920. Acta Apostolicae Sedis XIII (1921).

1048. BERTOGLIO, TOMMASO. *Missioni salesiane d'America.* Fossano: Tip. Rossetti, 1901.

1049. BISCEGLIA, JOHN B. *Italian Evangelical pioneers.* Kansas City: 1948.

1050. BONOMELLI, GEREMIA. *Lettera pastorale al clero e al popolo della sua diocesi.* Cremona: Tip. Foroni, 1896.

1051. BRANCHI, E. *Il primato degli italiani nella storia e nella civiltà americane. Breviario degli italiani in America.* Bologna: Cappelli, 1925.

1052. BROWNE, HENRY J. "The 'Italian problem' in the United States, 1880-1900," *U.S. Catholic Historical Society. Historical Records and Studies,* v. 35 (1946) pp. 46-72.

1053. CABRINI, FRANCESCA. *Viaggi della Madre Francesca Saverio Cabrini.* Torino: S.E.I., 1922.

1054. CALCAGNI, CHARLES P. *A sociological study of the religious change involving the Northern Italian in Barre, Vermont.* (Unpublished B.A. thesis. Bates College, 1954.)

1055. CALIARO, MARCO and MARIO L. FRANCESCONI. *Apostolo Degli Emigranti, Giovanni Battista Scalabrini.* Milano: Editrice Ancora, 1968.

1056. CAMIA, LORENZO. *Da Biella a S. Francisco di California, ossia storia di tre valligiani andornini in America.* Torino: Paravia, 1882.

1057. CAPITANI, PACIFICO. *La questione italiana negli Stati Uniti d'America. Condizione degli Italiani. Ragioni religiose sociali e politiche. Dal reverendo P. Capitani parroco della Colonia italiana di Cleveland, Ohio.* Cleveland: Milabe, 1891.

1058. CAPRA, GIUSEPPE. *I padri Scalabriniani nell' America del Nord.* San Benigno Canavese: Tipografia Don Bosco, 1916.

1059. CARUSO, JOSEPH. *The priest.* New York: Macmillan, 1956.

1060. "Catholic Italian losses," *Literary Digest,* v. 47 (October 11, 1913), p. 636.

1061. Charlton Street Memorial Church, New York. *Thirtieth anniversary of the religious and social work among the Italians of this community and the fifteenth anniversary of the Charlton Street Memorial Church, Sunday, May 22nd.* New York City: Printed by Società tipografica italiana, 1927.

1062. "Circular Letter of S. Consistorial Congregation of America Concerning the Care of Italian Emigrants." *The Ecclesiastical Review Year Book,* (1917), pp. 65-66.

1063. COLBACCHINI, PIETRO. *L'Associazione italiana di S. Raffaele a Patronato per gli emigranti.* Firenze: s.e., 1885.

1064. "Congregazione dei Missionari di S. Carlo per gli Italiani emigrati nelle Americhe," *Periodico mensile* (Piacenza, 1903-1905).

1065. "Congregazione. Lettera circolare ai vescovi d'America sulla cura degli emigranti italiani, Cum in varias Americas, 22 Febbraio 1915." *Acta Apostolicae Sedis VII* (1915).

1066. "Congregazione. Lettera circolare agli ecc. mi arcivescovi e vescovi di Calabria sulla costituzione di patronati ecclesiastici a pro degli emigranti, Assai gradite, 24 Novembre 1916." *Acta Apostolicae Sedis VIII* (1916).

1067. "Congregazione. Notificazione sulla cestituzione di un Pontificio Collegio di Sacerdoti per gli Italiani emigranti all' Estero, Sacerdotum Collegium, 26 Maggio 1921." *Acta Apostolicae Sedis XII* (1921).

1068. CONTE, GAETANO. *Le missioni protestanti e i nostri emigrati* Venezia: Tipografia dell' Istituto Industriale, 1906.

1069. CUSHING, RICHARD J. "Italian Immigrants," *Catholic Mind,* Vol. 52 (October 1954), pp. 604-609.

1070. DE LUCA, G. "Francesca Saverio Cabrini, la madre degli emigrati," *Nuova Antologia,* Vol. 394 (December 16, 1937), pp. 456-461.

1071. DI DOMENICA, A. "The sons of Italy in America," *Missionary Review of the World,* v. 41 (March 1918), pp. 189-195.

1072. DUMONT, COLEMAN. "Diocesan Bureau for the Care of Italian, Slav, Ruthenian, and Asiatic Catholics in America." *Ecclesiastical Review,* Vol. 48 (February 1913), pp. 221-222.

1073. FALESCHINI, GIOVANNI. *Leone XIII, gli emigranti e i socialisti.* Tolmezzo: Tip. Paschini, 1900.

1074. FELICI, ICILIO. *Father to the Immigrants, The Life of John Baptist Scalabrini,* New York: P.J. Kennedy & Sons, 1955.

1075. FEMMINELLA, FRANCIS X. "The Impact of Italian Migration and American Catholicism," *American Catholic Sociological Review,* vol. XXII (Fall 1961), p. 233-241.

1076. FRANCHI, F.J. "The Italian Catholic," *America,* vol. 44 (March 21, 1931), p. 584.

1077. FRANKLIN, LAURENCE. "The Italian in America: What he has been, what he shall be," *Catholic World,* vol. 71 (April 1900), pp. 72-73.

1078. *Golden Jubilee of the Leo House and St. Raphael Society in America, 1899-1939.* New York: Leo House, 1939.

1079. GREELEY, A.M. "Impact of Italian Migration and American Catholicism. Reply to F. Femminella." *American Catholic Sociological Review,* vol. 22 (Winter 1961), p. 333.

1080. GREGORI, VITTORIO. *Venticinque anni di Missione fra gli italiani immigrati de Boston, Mass.* (Milano: Tip. Bietti, 1913).

1081. GREGORI, VITTORIO. *Fiori sparsi di un gran vescovo, Mgr. Scalabrini.* Roma: Tip. Pallotta, 1908.

1082. GUGLIELMI, FRANCESCO. *The Italian Methodist mission in the Little Italy of Baltimore.* Seven years of evangelical Christian work. Baltimore: Printed by W.V. Guthrie, 1912.

1083. HACKETT, JANE K. *A Survey of Presbyterian Work with Italians in the Presbytery of Chicago.* [Unpublished M.A. thesis, Presbyterian College of Christian Education, Chicago, 1943].

1084. HILLENBRAND, M.J. "Has the Immigrant kept the Faith?" *America,* vol. 54 (November 23, 1935), pp. 153-155.

1085. HOFFMAN, GEORGE. *Catholic Immigrant Aid Societies in New York City from 1880 to 1920.* Unpublished doctoral thesis, St. John's University, 1947. [Chapters on the Italians]

1086. IACHINI, CARLO. *La mia prima missione nel Nord America, 1904-1908.* Recanati: Tip. Carelli, 1910.

1087. "Italians in America," *Tablet* [London], vol. 180 (October 17, 1942), p. 186.

1088. JONES, H.D. *The evangelical movement among Italians in New York City.* New York: Committee of the Federation of Churches of Greater New York and the Brooklyn Church and Mission Federation, 1933-34.

1089. KELLY, MARY GILBERT. "The Catholic Charities and the Italian Auxiliary," *La Voce dell' Emigrato,* vol. 6, (April 1929), pp. 11-12.

1090. LAGNESE, J.G. "Italian Catholic," *America,* vol. 44 (February 21, 1931), pp. 475-476. Discussion. *America,* vol. 44 (March, 21, 1931), pp. 583-584.

1091. *La Società San Raffaele per la protezione degli immigranti italiani in Boston, New York,* 1906.

1092. LE BERTHON, T. "Apostolate to Italo-Americans," *Catholic Mind,* vol. 51, (April 1953), pp. 211-219.

1093. LE BERTHON, T. "Life of Luigi," *Catholic Digest,* vol. 19 (January 1955), pp. 93-96.

1094. "Letter of Pope Leo XIII," *The American Ecclesiastical Review,* vol. 1, (February 1889), pp. 45-48.

1095. LYNCH, D. "The religious condition of Italians in New York," *America,* vol. 10 (March 21, 1914).

1096. MACKEY, U.L. "A Venture in cooperation; how they built the Italian branch of the Webb Horton Church, Middleton, N.Y.," *Missionary Review,* v. 10 (August 1917), pp. 595-597.

1097. McLEOD, CHRISTIAN. [Anna C. Ruddy]. *The Heart of the Stranger. A Story of Little Italy.* New York: Fleming H. Revell Co., 1908. [The life of Italians in East Harlem, New York City, written by a social/religious reformer who founded the Home Garden (1901) later to become LaGuardia Memorial House.] See No. 447.

1098. MANGANO, ANTONIO. "The associated life of the Italians in New York City," *Charities,* v. 12 (May 7, 1904), pp. 476-482.

1099. MANGANO, ANTONIO. *Religious work for Italians in America: A Handbook for Leaders in Missionary Work.* New York: Immigrant Work Committee of the Home Missions Council [c. 1915].

1100. MANGANO, ANTONIO. *Sons of Italy: a social and religious study of the Italians in America.* New York: Missionary Education Movement of the United States and Canada, 1917. Reprinted with A Foreword by F. Cordasco, New York: Russell & Russell, 1972.

1101. MARIANO, GABRIEL. *History of Our Lady of Loretto Day Nursery,* [Unpublished typewritten MS.], New York: Our Lady of Loretto Nursery, 1941.

1102. MILESI, F. *Mons. Scalabrini e il problema dell' assistenza agli emigrati,* [Academic thesis presented at Università Cattolica del S. Cuore. Milano, 1965-1966].

1103. *Missioni scalabriniane in America. Mongrafia.* Roma: Tip. Poliglotta, 1939. See also, G. Bortolucci, *Una rassegna dell' oppuscolo di Mons. Scalabrini sopra l'emigrazione italiana in America.* Modena: Tip. Rossi, 1887. See No. 1055.

1104. MONDELLO, SALVATORE. "Protestant Proselytism among the Italians in the U.S.A. as Reported in American Magazines," *Social Sciences,* vol. 41 (April 1966), pp. 84-90.

1105. MURPHY, [Sister] MARY C. *Bishop Joseph Rosati, C.M., and the Diocese of New Orleans.* Unpublished doctoral thesis, St. Louis University, 1961.

1106. NOA, T.L. "Religion and good citizenship," *Vital Speeches*, v. 19 (October 15, 1952), pp. 29-32.

1107. PALMIERI, AURELIO. "Italian protestantism in the United States," *Catholic World*, v. 107 (May 1918), pp. 177-189.

1108. PALMIERI, AURELIO. "Il clero italiano negli Stati Uniti," *Vita Italiana*, v. 15 (1920), pp. 113-127.

1109. PALMIERI, AURELIO. *Il Grave Problema Religioso Italiano negli Stati Uniti.* Florence, 1921. [major work]

1110. PELOSO, ROCCO. "A Short History of the Mission." Loretto Club of the Mission of Our Lady of Loretto, *Club Notes*, vol. 6 (December 1916), pp. 38-47.

1111. PICCINNI, GAETANO. *Blessed Frances Xavier Cabrini in America.* [Unpublished M.A. thesis, Columbia University, 1942]

1112. PISTELLA, DOMENICO. *La Madonna del Carmine e gli Italiani d'America.* New York, 1954.

1113. PIUS PP. X. "Lettera al venerabile fratello Giovanni Maria Arcivescovo di New York, *Haud its pridem*, 26 Febbraio 1904," *PII X. Acta I (1905).*

1114. PIUS PP. X. "Lettera al Sacerdote Don Domenico Vicentini, Direttore dell' Istituto di San Carlo per gli Italiani emigranti, Vehementer nobis, 4 Settembre 1913," *Acta Apostolicae Sedis IV (1912).*

1115. PIUS PP. XI. "Lettera apostolica con cui si dichiara beata la serva di Dio Francesca Saveria Cabrini, Benignus Deus, 13 Novembre 1938," *Acta Apostolicae Sedis XXXI (1938).*

1116. PIUS PP. XII. "Lettera decretale con cui si decretano gli onori degli altari alla beata Francesca Saveria Cabrini, Fondatrice dell' Istituto delle Missionarie del S. Cuore di Gesu, Spiritus Domini, 7 Luglio 1946," *Acta Apostolicae Sedis XXXIX (1946).*

1117. PIUS PP. XII. "Costitutzione apostolica sulla cura spirituale degli emigranti, Exsul Familia, l'Agosto 1952," *Acta Apostolicae Sedis XXXXIV (1952).*

1118. *Questione scolastica negli Stati Uniti e la decisione della propaganda.* Roma: Tip. Sociale, 1892.

1119. *Rapporto dell' Società di San Raffaele Arcangelo per la protezione degli italiani immigranti, Boston, Mass., 1802-1904.* Boston: La Societa, 1905.

1120. REYNOLDS, MINNIE J. "The Italian and his church at home," *Congregational Home Missionary Society*, n.p. n.d.

1121. ROBINSON, GILBERT K. "Catholic birth-rate: further facts and implications," *American Journal of Sociology*, v. 41 (May 1936), pp. 757-766.

1122. Roman Catholic Archdiocese of New York. *Archives*. [Invaluable primary sources, many in Italian.] *Cf.*, also *Archives, Catholic dioceses of Brooklyn, Boston, Providence, Newark, Chicago, Philadelphia, etc.*

1123. ROSSI, PAOLO A. "I miei cinque anni di missione in New Orleans," *La Voce coloniale, 1931.*

1124. RUSSO, NICHOLAS. *The Religious Acculturation of the Italians in New York City*. Unpublished doctoral thesis, St. John's University, 1968. [See revised version in No. 423]

1125. SARTORIO, HENRY C. "Work Among Italians," *The Churchman* (September 1, 1917), p. 273.

1126. SARTORIO, ENRICO C. *Social and religious life of Italians in America.* Boston: The Christopher Publishing House, 1918.

1127. SCHICK, R. "Father Bandini: missionary in the Ozarks," *Ave Maria*, vol. 66 (December 1947), pp. 782-786.

1128. SCHRIVER, WILLIAM P. *At work with the Italians.* New York; Missionary Education Movement of the United States and Canada, 1917.

1129. SCHRIVER, WILLIAM P. "Evangelical movement among Italians," *Missionary Review*, v. 58 (January, 1935), p. 5.

1130. St. Louis, St. Ambrose Church. *Nuova chiesa italiana di Sant' Ambrogio dedicata il 27 Giugno, 1926.* St. Louis, 1926.

1131. St. Louis, St. Ambrose Catholic School. *Souvenir program of the jubilee celebrations in honor of Father Lupo for the benefit of St. Ambrose School, Sunday, August 8-15, 1937.* (St. Louis, 1937).

1132. St. Louis. St. Anthony of Padua Church. *Souvenir of the diamond jubilee of St. Anthony parish, 1933-1938.* Saint Louis, Missouri. St. Louis, 1938.

1133. St. Louis. St. Ambrose Church. *Fortieth anniversary. A historical review, sketches and data of St. Ambrose Parish. Past and present achievements by Italians in America, 1913-1943.* St. Louis, 1943.

1134. TANGARONE, ADAM. *An intensive study of the Torrington Italian Mission connected with the Center Congregational Church, Torrington, Conn.* [Unpublished M.R.E. thesis, Hardford School of Religious Education, 1935.]

1135. TESSAROLO, G. *Exsul Familia: The Church's Magna Charta for Migrants*. Staten Island, New York: St. Charles Seminary, 1962.

1136. TESTA, STEFANO L. "Strangers from Rome in Greater New York," *Missionary Review of the World*, v. 31 (March, 1908), pp. 216-218.

1137. TOLINO, JOHN V. "Solving the Italian Problem," *Ecclesiastical Review*, vol. 99 (September 1938), pp. 246-256.

1138. TOLINO, JOHN V. "The future of the Italian-American problem," *Ecclesiastical Review*, v. 101 (September, 1939), pp. 221-232.

1139. TOLINO, JOHN V. "Church in America and the Italian Problem," *Ecclesiastical Review*, vol. 101 (January 1939), pp. 22-32.

1140. TOLINO, JOHN V. "Priest in the Italian Problem," *Ecclesiastical Review*, vol. 109 (November 1943), pp. 321-330.

1141. TOMASI, SILVANO M. "The Ethnic Church and the Integration of Italian Immigrants in the United States," S.M. Tomasi and M.H. Engel, *The Italian Experience in the United States* (Staten Island, New York: Center for Migration Studies, 1970), pp. 163-193. [important statement. *Cf.*, No. 1142.]

1142. VECOLI, RUDOLPH J. "Prelates and Peasants: Italian Immigrants and the Catholic Church," *Journal of Social History*, vol. 2 (Spring 1969), pp. 217-268. [considerable bibliography]

1143. VIAN, NELLO. *Madre Cabrini: the life of Mother Cabrini and her work in the United States.* Brescia: Morcelliana, 1938.

1144. VINCENTINI, D. *L'Apostolo degli italiani emigranti nelle Americhe,* (Piacenza, 1909).

1145. WALSH, JAMES J. "An apostle of the Italians," *Catholic World*, v. 107 (April 1918), pp. 64-71.

1146. WILLIAMS, PHYLLIS H. *The religious mores of the South-Italians of New Haven.* Unpublished M.A., thesis, Yale University, 1933.

1147. WRIGHT, FRED H. "Italian in America," *Missionary Review*, v. 30 (March 1907), pp. 196-198.

1148. WRIGHT, FRED H. "The composite Italian," *World Outlook*, v. 3 (October 1917), pp. 22-23.

1149. WRIGHT, FRED H. *The Italians in America.* New York: Missionary Education Movement, 1913.

1150. WUNSCH, PAUL I. "The Italian Catholic," *America,* vol. 41 (March 21, 1931), p. 584.

E. Crime, Delinquency, and Social Deviance

1151. ABBOTT, E. "Statistica relativa alla criminalità e all' immigrazione in Chicago." *Bollettino dell' Emigrazione (1915).*

1152. ANDERSON, ROBERT T. "From Mafia to Casa Nostra," *American Journal of Sociology,* vol. 71 (November 1965), pp. 302-310.

1153. BENNET, W.S. "Immigrants and Crime," *Annals. American Academy of Political and Social Science,* v. 34 (1909), pp. 117-124.

1154. "Blackmail and murder," *Outlook,* v. 91 (March 27, 1909), pp. 656-657.

1155. "Black Hand sway in Italian New York," *Literary Digest,* v. 47 (August 20, 1913), pp. 308-310.

1156. BOSCO, AUGUSTO. *L'omicidio negli Stati Uniti d'America.* Roma: Bertero, 1887.

1157. BRAUN, MARCUS. "Report [concerning certain knowledge believed to be possessed by the Italian authorities as to emigration of undesirable aliens to the United States, and also in regard to inadmissible aliens to Vera Cruz en route to points in the United States]," *U.S. Bureau of Immigration. Annual Report of Commissioner-general.* 1903, pp. 86-96.

1158. CIRAOLO, G. "La delinquenza degli italiani all' Estero. *Italia coloniale* (1901).

1159. CLAGHORN, KATE H. "Immigration in its Relation to Pauperism." *American Academy of Political and Social Science Annals,* vol. XXIV (July - December 1904), pp. 187-205.

1160. COLAJANNI, NAPOLEONE. "La Criminalità degli Italiani negli Stati Uniti," in *Gli Italiani negli Stati Uniti.* Roma: Presso la Rivista Popolare 1906.

1161. COLAJANNI, NAPOLEONE. "La criminalità degli italiani negli Stati Uniti," *Nuova Antologia,* v. 145 (February 15, 1910), pp. 693-712.

1162. COLAJANNI, NAPOLEONE. "Sulle condizioni che favoriscono la criminalità degli Italiani negli Stati Uniti d'America," *Rivista contemporanea* (Febbraio 1910).

1163. COXE, JOHN E. "The New Orleans Mafia Incident," *Louisiana Historical Quarterly,* vol. 20 (1937), p. 1066.

1164. D'AMATO, GAETANO. "The black hand myth," *North American Review,* v. 187 (April 1908), pp. 543-549.

1165. "Death of Joseph Petrosino," *Current Literature,* v. 46 (1909), pp. 478-480.

1166. DENISON, L. "Black hand," *Everybody's Magazine,* v. 19 (1908), pp. 291-301.

1167. FIASCHETTI, MICHAEL. *You gotta be rough: the adventures of detective Fiaschetti of the Italian Squad* (as told to Prosper Buranelli). New York: Doubleday, Doran, 1930.

1168. FINESTONE, H. "Reformation and recidivism among Italian and Polish criminal offenders," *American Journal of Sociology,* vol. 72 (May 1967), pp. 575-588.

1169. FRASCA, DOM. *King of Crime.* New York: Devon, 1959. [Vito Genovese.]

1170. GASTER, D.F. "Report," *Foreign Relations of the United States 1891,* pp. 706-711. [Lynching of Italians in Louisiana.]

1171. HOWERTH, I.A. "Are the Italians a dangerous Class?" *Charities Review,* vol. 4 (November 1894).

1172. IANNI, FRANCIS A.J. "The Mafia and the Web of Kinship," *The Public Interest,* (Winter 1971), pp. 78-100. [a major contribution]

1173. "Italian Criminals: the Cosa Nostra," *America,* vol. 109 (October 26, 1963), p. 474.

1174. *Italian white hand in Chicago.* Chicago, Tip. dell' Italia, 1908. See also, *Italian white hand in Chicago (Illinois Studies. Actions and Results (1906).*

1175. LANDESCO, JOHN. "Crime and the Failure of Institutions in Chicago's Immigrant Areas," *Journal of the American Institute of Criminal Law and Criminology,* vol. 23 (July - August, 1932). pp. 239-240.

1176. MARIANO, JOHN H. *The Italian immigrant and our courts.* Boston: Christopher, 1925.

1177. MARR, ROBERT H. "The New Orleans Mafia Case," *American Law Review,* Vol. 25 (1891), pp. 414-431.

1178. MOSCA, GAETANO. "Mafia," *Encyclopedia of the Social Sciences,* (1937). [Important article by leading Italian sociologist]

1179. MORGAN, A. "What shall we do with the dago? Prisons should not be comfortable," *Popular Science Monthly*, v. 38 (December 1890), pp. 172-179. Reply by W. H. Larrabee, *Popular Science Monthly*, v. 38 (February 1891), pp. 553-554.

1180. "Murders and mysteries of Kansas City's Little Italy," *Literary Digest*, v. 61 (April 5, 1919), pp. 51-55.

1181. NELLI, HUMBERT S. "Italians and crime in Chicago: the formative years, 1890-1920," *American Journal of Sociology*, vol. 74 (January 1969), pp. 373-391. See No. 664.

1182. OPPENHEIMER, FRANCIS. "The truth about the black hand," *The Denver Republican,* January 17, 1909.

1183. PIERANTONI, AUGUSTO. "I linciaggi negli Stati Uniti e la emigrazione italiana," *L 'Italia coloniale,* v. 1 (April-May 1904), pp. 423-447; v. 2 (July 1904), pp. 34-52.

1184. RADIN, E.D. "Detective in a derby hat: Petrosino who broke the power of the Black Hand in Little Italy," *New York Times Magazine,* March 12, 1944.

1185. REID, SIDNEY. "The death sign," *Independent,* v. 70 (April 6, 1911), pp. 711-715.

1186. SASSONE, TOMMASO. "Italy's criminals in the United States," *Current History,* v. 15 (October 1921), pp. 23-31.

1187. Society for Italian immigrants [New York]. How *Salvatore Zamanti, an Italian immigrant was swindled. A series of documents.* New York, 1904.

1188. SCHIAVO, GIOVANNI E. "What crime statistics show about Italians," *Italian Historical Society* (1930).

1189. SCHIAVO, GIOVANNI E. *The truth about the Mafia and Organized Crime in America.* New York: Vigo Press, 1962.

1190. SPERANZA, GINO. "Petrosino and the Black hand." *Survey,* v. 22 (1909), pp. 11-14.

1191. TALESE, GUY. "The Ethics of Frank Costello," *Esquire,* (September 1961); also, "Joe Bonanno," *Ibid.* (Aug., Sept., Oct., 1971) ["Joe Bananas"]; also, *Honor Thy Father.* New York: World, 1971.

1192. "The Black hand scourge," *Cosmopolitan,* v. 47 (June 1909), pp. 31-41.

1193. "The Talk of the Town," *New Yorker*, vol. 26 (November 4, 1950), p. 37. [Costello and Luciano and influence in New York politics.]

1194. "To rid this country of foreign criminals," *Harper's Weekly*, v. 52 (June 27, 1908), p. 16.

1195. TRAIN, ARTHUR. "Imported Crime: the story of the Camorra in America," *McClure's*, v. 39 (1912), pp. 82-94.

1196. TYLER, GUS. "The Mafia," *Organized crime in America*. Ann Arbor: The University of Michigan Press, 1962.

1197. "Undesirable citizens," *Independent*, v. 66 (April 1, 1909), 712-713.

1198. WHITE, FRANK M. "Fostering foreign criminals," *Harper's Weekly*, v. 53 (May 8, 1909), pp. 7-8.

1199. WHITE, FRANK M. "How the United States fosters the Black Hand," *Outlook*, v. 93 (October 30, 1909), pp. 495-500.

1200. WHITE, FRANK M. "A man who was unafraid," [Petrosino]. *Harper's Weekly*, v. 53 (March 27, 1909), p. 8.

1201. WHITE, FRANK M. "Against the Black Hand," *Collier's Weekly*, v. 45 (September 3, 1910), p. 19.

1202. WHITE, FRANK M. "Against the Black Hand," *Collier's Weekly*, v. 45 (September 19. 1910), p. 19.

1203. WHITE, FRANK M. "Black Hand. in control of Italian New York," *Outlook*, v. 104 (August 16, 1913), pp. 857-65.

1204. WARNER, ARTHUR H. "Amputating the Black Hand," *Survey*, v. 22 (May 1, 1909), pp. 166-167.

1205. WATCHORN, ROBERT. "The Black Hand and the Immigrant," *Outlook*, v. 92 (July 31, 1909), pp. 794-797.

1206. WOODS, ARTHUR. "The 'Black Hand' problem in America," *Review of Reviews*, v. 39 (1909), pp. 627-628.

1207. WOODS, ARTHUR. "The Problem of the Black Hand," *McClure's Magazine*, v. 33, no. 1 (May 1909), pp. 40-47.

V. THE ITALIAN AMERICAN IN THE POLITICO-ECONOMIC CONTEXT

    A. *Labor and the Padrone System*
    B. *Politics and Government*
    C. *Agriculture [Rural Settlement]*

V.   THE ITALIAN AMERICAN IN THE POLITICO-ECONOMIC CONTEXT

The padrone system has received considerable attention, and a good point to begin its study is with Marie Lipari (No. 1241) who argues that the system grew out of the economic structure of the United States and the earlier practices of apprenticeship and indentured service. As yet, no adequate treatment of Italian Americans in the contexts of American labor history has appeared, and most of the available literature provides points of departure for still further study: it is an irony that an unusually able American academician has given his major attention to the study of Italians and the Argentine labor movement, and has only tangentially dealt with the Italian experience in the United States. (Samuel L. Baily, No. 1212). The vast literature on Italians in American politics and government (both ephemeral and substantive) is only very broadly represented in the titles which have been collected: they range from the impressive studies of Fiorello H. LaGuardia by Professor Arthur Mann to the portrait sketches of political leaders in the popular press. An excellent overview is in the trenchant paper by Dr. Salvatore J. LaGumina (No. 1308). The settlement of Italians on the land and the agricultural experience is curiously analogous (if not directly parallel in development) to the efforts to settle Jewish immigrants on the land best exemplified in the efforts of Baron de Hirsch, but unlike the Jewish experience, the Italian experience remains to be written:* how rich the Italian adventure on the land has been is amply attested to by the work of Andrew F. Rolle (No. 416).

A.   *Labor And The Padrone System*

1208. ACRITELLI, PIETRO.   "Il contributo degli Italiani alla prosperità materiale della città di New York," *Italia Coloniale* (Gennaio - Febbraio, 1904).

1209. AMICO, SALVATORE.   *Gli italiani e l'Internazionale dei sarti da donna. Racolta di storie e memorie contemporanee.* Mamaroneck, N.Y., 1944.

1210. "An American revival of an ancient craft: Italian embroidery," *Outlook,* v. 96 (1910), pp. 800-801.

1211. ANTONINI, LUIGI.   *Dynamic democracy.* New York: Eloquent Press, 1944. [Compiled by the Italian Labor Education Bureau for the 24th anniversary of Local 89].

---

*As a model in ethnic historiography, see Samuel Joseph, *History of the Baron de Hirsch Fund* (New York: Jewish Publication Society, 1935).

1212. BAILY, SAMUEL L. "The Italians and Organized Labor in the United States and Argentina: 1880-1910," *International Migration Review,* vol. I, New Series (Summer 1967), pp. 56-66.

1213. BONFIGLIO, SEBASTIANO. *Vita coloniale. Il banchiere italiano nel Nord America.* Brooklyn: Louis Dimola, 1911.

1214. BOUTET, FEDERIGO. "Istituti di patronato dell' emigrazione italiana negli Stati Uniti," *L'Italia coloniale,* vol. I (June 1903), pp. 574-580.

1215. CARPENTER, NILES. "On their way; the implacable optimism of the immigrant worker," *Survey,* v. 56 (July 15, 1926), pp. 453-454.

1216. CHANDLER, WILLIAM. "Resolution calling for statement on Padrone system," *53 Congress, 2nd Session. Senate Misc. Doc. 207,* v. 5 (June 11, 1894).

1217. CLAGHORN, KATE H. "The Italian under economic stress," *Charities,* v. 12 (May 7, 1907), pp. 501-504.

1218. CIOLLI, DOMINIC T. "The 'Wop' in the track gang," *Immigrants in America Review,* v. 11 (July 1916), pp. 61-64.

1219. CRAWFORD, JOHN S. *Luigi Antonini, His Influence on Italian American Relations.* New York, 1959.

1220. D'ALESSANDRE, JOHN J. "Occupational trends of Italians in New York City," *Italy-America Monthly,* v. 2 (February 25, 1935), pp. 11-21. *Casa Italiana Educational Bureau,* Bulletin No. 8, 1935.

1221. DANA, JULIAN. *Giant in the West.* New York, 1947. [On A.P. Giannini]

1222. DITTA G. TUOTI & C. *La proprietà fondiaria degli italiani nella Greater di New York.* New York: Tip. Rossotti, 1906.

1223. ERICKSON, CHARLOTTE. *American Industry and the European Immigrant.* Cambridge. Harvard University Press, 1957.

1224. FENTEN, EDWIN. *Immigrants and Unions, A Case Study: Italians and American Labor, 1870-1920.* Unpublished doctoral thesis, Harvard University, 1957.

1225. FENTON, EDWIN. "Italians in the labor movement," *Pennsylvania History,* v. 26, no. 2 (April 1959), pp. 133-148.

1226. FENTON, EDWIN. "Italian Workers in the Stone Workers Union," *Labor History,* vol. 3 (Spring 1962), pp. 188-207.

1227. GHIRADELLA, ROMEO. *The social organization of work among the Italians in New York City.* Unpublished M.A. thesis, Columbia University, 1929.

1228. GIOVINCO, JOSEPH. "Democracy in Banking: Bank of Italy and California's Italians," *California Historical Society Quarterly,* (September 1968).

1229. GRECO, VINCENZO. *Il Banco di Napoli e la sua funzione negli Stati Uniti.* Carrara, 1904.

1230. HALE, E.E. "Italians in Boston; the padrone question," *Lend a Hand,* v. 12 (1893), pp. 449+.

1231. HARTT, ROLLIN L. "Made in Italy; the story of what is happening in the largest Italian city in the world–New York," *Independent,* v. 106 (July 23, 1921), pp. 19-20, 36-37.

1232. "I lavoratori italiani nel West Virginia," *L'Italia coloniale,* v. 2 (August - September 1903), pp. 858-861.

1233. *Influence of Padrone.* Report of Commission of Immigration, State of New York. New York, 1909, pp. 14, 122.

1234. IORIZZO, LUCIANO JOHN. *Italian Immigration and the Impact of the Padrone System.* Unpublished doctoral thesis. Syracuse University, 1966.

1235. IORIZZO, LUCIANO J. "The Padrone and immigrant distribution," S.M. Tomasi and M.H. Engel, eds., *The Italian Experience in the United States* (Staten Island, N.Y.: Center for Migration Studies, 1970), pp. 43-75.

1236. IRWIN, ELISABETH A. "The story of a transplanted industry; lace workers of the Italian quarter in New York," *Craftsman,* v. 12 (1907), pp. 404-409.

1237. JOSEPHSON, MATTHEW. "Big Bull of the West," *Saturday Evening Post,* vol. 220 (September 13, 1947), p. 15+. [A.P. Giannini]

1238. KOREN, JOHN. "The padrone system and the padrone banks," *U.S. Bureau of Labor. Special Bulletin* No. 9 (March 1897), pp. 113-129.

1239. LATHROP, M.D. "Section Boss," *Common Ground,* vol. 3 (1943), pp. 80-85.

1240. LELAND, W.G. "Black vs. Italian labor [Letter to the editor]," *Nation,* v. 82 (February 1, 1906), p. 97.

1241. LIPARI, MARIE. "The Padrone System: an aspect of American economic history," *Italy-America Monthly*, vol. 2 (April 1935), pp. 4-10.

1242. MASTROGIOVANNI, SALVATORE. *Le prime società di patronato per gli emigranti negli Stati Uniti ed in Italia.* Venezia: Tip. dell' Istituto industriale, 1906.

1243. MONTALBO, ORAZIO. *Diciannove anni di vita e di lotta: appunti e riccordi, 1905-1924. Banca; industria; lavoro.* Relazione fatta al primo congresso fascistà negli Stati Uniti tenuto a Philadelphia, 17 Ottobre 1925. Brooklyn, New York: Guerriero, 1925.

1244. MURPHY, MARK. "Profiles," *New Yorker,* (May 15, 1943), p. 25+. [Career of Patsy D'Agostino, supermarket tycoon.]

1245. NELLI, HUMBERT. "The Italian Padrone System in the United States." *Labor History*, vol. 5 (Spring 1964), pp. 153-167.

1246. ODENCRANTZ, LOUISE C. *Italian women in industry: a study of conditions in New York City.* New York: Russell Sage Foundation, 1919.

1247. *Padrone system.* Facts in regard to the padrone system in the United States. June 20, 1894. 53 Congress, 2nd session. Senate Document. No. 114, v. 4.

1248. *Padrone system and common labor.* U.S. Industrial Commission, v. 5, pp. 430-446.

1249. PHIPARD, CHARLES B. "The philanthropist padrone," *Charities,* v. 12 (May 7, 1904), pp. 470-472.

1250. ROSSETTI-AGRESTI O. "Gli operai americani e l'emigrazione italiana," *Nuova Antologia* (Ottobre 1909).

1251. ROSSI, ALESSANDRO. "Immigranti nelle città. L'Ufficio del lavoro a Washington e le classi rurali," *Rassegna Nazionale* (1897).

1252. ROSSI, E. "Istituti di patronato dell' emigrazione italiana negli Stati Uniti," *Bollettino dell' emigrazione* (1903).

1253. "Sedicenti banchieri negli Stati Uniti," *Bollettino degli Affari Esteri* (1897).

1254. SHERIDAN, FRANK J. "Italian, Slavic and Hungarian unskilled immigrant laborers in the U.S.," *U.S. Bureau of Labor Bulletin,* vol. 15 (September 1907), pp. 403-486.

1255. SIMBOLI, CESIDIO. "When the boss went too far," *World Outlook,* v. 3 (October 1917), pp. 19-20, 28+.

1256. SPADONI, ADRIANA. "Italian working women in New York," *Collier's*, v. 49 (March 23, 1912), pp. 14-15.

1257. STEPHANS, HERBERT L. "American Tobacco Head Gives his sales, advertising philosophy," *Printer's Ink*, vol. 225 (November 12, 1948), p. 33+. [The Sicilian immigrant background of Vincent Riggio, President of the American Tobacco Company].

1258. SPERANZA, GINO C. "Forced labor in West Virginia," *Outlook*, v. 74 (1903), pp. 407-410.

1259. SPERANZA, GINO C. "The Italian foreman as a social agent," *Charities*, v. 11 (July 4, 1903), pp. 26-28.

1260. VITI, ALONZO. "Commercio a Filadelfia con l'Italia. Rapporto," *Bollettino Consolare*, (Octtobre 1869).

1261. ZUCCA ANTONIO. "La relazione del presidente alla Camera di commercio italiana di New York," *L'Italia coloniale*, v. 2 (August - September, 1903), pp. 866-870.

B. *Politics and Government*

1262. "America and Italy," *Spectator,* v. 66 (April 4, 1891), pp. 466-467.

1263. AURITI, FRANCESCO.   *Questioni giuridiche tra l'Italia e la Federazione Americana per i fatti di Nuova Orleans.* Roma: E. Loescher, 1898.

1264. BARONE, C.   "Dual Nationality with particular reference to the legal status of the Italo-Americans," *Fordham Law Review,* vol. 23 (December 1954), pp. 243-295.

1265. BONE, HUGH A.   "Political Parties in New York City," *The American Political Science Review,* April 1946. [Material on Italians in New York City politics.]

1266. BOSCARINI, GIOVANNI.   *Fascismo dalla marcia su Roma all' impero.* Boston: Peabody Press, 1937.

1267. BRUNER, J. and J. SAYRE.   "Shortwave listening in an Italian Community; study of Boston's Italian North end," *Public Opinion Quarterly,* vol. 5, No. 4 (December 1941), pp. 640-656.

1268. CIAMPIS, MARIO DE.   "Note sul movimento socialistà tra gli emigrati italiani negli U.S.A. (1890-1921)," *Cronache meridionali* [Napoli], anno 6 (April 1959), pp. 255-273.

1269. CLARK, ELEANOR.   "Press goes to war; II. Italian press, New York," *New Republic,* v. 84 (November 6, 1935), pp. 356-357.

1270. "Concerning the exemption of Italian aliens from alien enemy classification," *Interpreter Releases,* vol. 19 (October 20, 1942), pp. 353-362.

1271. *Correspondence in relation to the killing of prisoners in* New Orleans on March 14, 1891. Washington, D.C.: Government Printing Office, 1891.

1272. *Correspondence in relation to lawless killing of Italian laborers in Colorado.* February 3, 1896. 54th Congress, 1st session. House Document No. 195, v. 53.

1273. COXE, JOHN E.   "The New Orleans Mafia incident," *Louisiana Historical Quarterly,* v. 20 (1937), pp. 1066-1110. (Bibl. pp. 1109-1110).

1274. CRISCUOLO, LUIGI.   *Articles on the Italo-America entente and Kindred subjects.* New York, 1925.

1275. CRISCUOLO, LUIGI. *An Italo-American looks at Britain: an open letter to His Excellency the Rt. Hon. Lord Halifax.* New York, 1941.

1276. CRISCUOLO, LUIGI. *Fifth columnists and their friends in and out of Congress, with my particular respect to Emanuel Celler, M.C., distinguished member of the New York Bar: an open letter to the members of the 77th Congress.* New York, 1942.

1277. CRISCUOLO, LUIGI. *"Il Mondo and the mercenaries of Karl Marx & Co.:* complimentary supplement for the readers of *Il Mondo* for February 1942: a reply to the leading article in that issue, entitled: Luigi Criscuolo, a fascist in citizen's disguise." New York, 1942.

1278. CUPELLI, ALBERTO. "The U.S. Italian Language Press Dances to the Nazi Tune," *Il Mondo,* VII (March 1944), p. 3.

1279. DIGGINS, J.P. "Italo-American and anti-Fascist opposition," *Journal of American History,* vol. 54 (December 1967), pp. 579-598.

1280. DODD, BELLA. *School of Darkness.* New York: Devin, 1963. [Autobiography of Bella Visono]

1281. DOS PASSOS, JOHN. "Carlo Tresca," *Nation,* vol. 159 (January 23, 1943), p. 123.

1282. DUFFIELD, MARCUS. "Mussolini's American empire: the fascist invasion of the United States," *Harper's Magazine,* v. 159 (November 1929), pp. 661-672.

1283. DUFFIELD, MARCUS. "Mussolini's red herring," *Nation,* v. 129 (November 29, 1929), p. 644.

1284. EASTMAN, MAX. "Profile: Troublemaker," *New Yorker,* vol. 10 (September 15, 1934), p. 31 [Carlo Tresca].

1285. EGAN, LEO. "The How and Why of DeSapio," *New York Times Magazine,* (September 14, 1958), p. 25+.

1286. ELLIOT, WILLIAM Y. *Why tolerate Mussolini's agents?* Washington, D.C.: American Council on Public Affairs, 1940.

1287. "Fascism at Columbia University; Casa Italiana and the Italian department," *Nation,* v. 139 (November 7, 1934), pp. 523-524; 530-531. *Discussion:* v. 139: pp. 550-552; 565; 590 (November 14-21, 1934); v. 140: pp. 117; 129-130; 377-378; 388 (January 30; April 3, 1935). *School & Society,* v. 40 (November 24, 1934), pp. 695-698.

1288. "Fascismo in America," *The Interpreter,* v. 2 (May 1923), pp. 3-8.

1289. FRANZONI, AUSONIO. *Gli Italiani d'America e la cittadinanza.* Roma: Tipografia cooperativa sociale, 1923.

1290. "From Dazzling to Fizzling," *Time,* vol. 84 (October 23, 1964), [Foster Furcolo].

1291. GHIO, PAUL. *L'anarchisme aux Etats Unis.* Paris: Colin, 1903. [material on Italian anarchists.]

1292. [Giuseppe Defina.] *Report relating to claims of Giuseppe Defina in connection with lynching of Italian subjects at Tallulah, La.* [July 20, 1899]. 57th Congress, 1st session. Senate Documents no. 95, v. 8 (4226).

1293. "G.O.P. Faces with a Future," *Newsweek,* vol. 57 (June 12, 1961), p. 31 [John Volpe].

1294. HANIGHEN, FRANK C. "Foreign political movements in the U.S.," *Foreign Affairs,* v. 16 (October 1937), pp. 1-20; pp. 11-16 [Italians].

1295. HAVEMANN, ERNEST. "Man with his bag Packed," *Life.* (March 19, 1951), p. 85 [On Michael V. DiSalle].

1296. HAWLEY, CAMERON. "New Territory for a New Style Boss," *Life,* (June 6, 1955), pp. 157-174 [Closeup on Carmine DeSapio].

1297. HEILBRONER, ROBERT. "Carmine G. DeSapio: The Smile on the Face of the Tiger," *Harper's Magazine,* vol. 209 (July 1954), pp. 23-33.

1298. KARLIN, ALEXANDER J. *The Italo-American Incident of 1891.* Unpublished doctoral thesis, University of Minnesota, 1941.

1299. KARLIN, ALEXANDER J. "New Orleans lynching of 1891 and the American press," *Louisiana Historical Quarterly,* v. 24 (1941), pp. 187-204.

1300. KARLIN, ALEXANDER J. "The Italo American incident of 1891 and the road to reunion," *Journal of Southern History,* v. 8 (May 1942), pp. 242-246.

1301. KARLIN, ALEXANDER J. "Some repercussions of the New Orleans Mafia incident of 1891," *Research Studies of the State College of Washington, Pullman, Washington,* v. 11 (December 1943), pp. 267-282.

1302. KENDALL, JOHN S. "Patti in New Orleans," *Southwest Review,* v. 16 (July 1931), pp. 460.

1303. *Killing of certain laborers in Colorado.* 54th Congress, 1st session. House Documents, v. 53.

1304. *Killing of Italian subjects at Erwin, Mass.* [July 11, 1901]. Message of the President. 57th Congress, 2nd session, v. 5

1305. LaGUMINA, SALVATORE J. *Vito Marcantonio, Labor and the New Deal, 1935-1940.* Unpublished doctoral thesis, St. John's University, 1966.

1306. LaGUMINA, SALVATORE J., ed. *Ethnicity in American Political Life: The Italian American Experience.* New York: American Italian Historical Association, 1968.

1307. LaGUMINA, SALVATORE J. *Vito Marcantonio.* Dubuque, Iowa: Kendall-Hunt, 1969.

1308. LaGUMINA, SALVATORE J. "Case Studies of Ethnicity and Italo-American Politicians," S.M. Tomasi and M.H. Engel, eds. *The Italian Experience in the United States* (Staten Island, N.Y.: Center for Migration Studies, 1970), pp. 143-161.

1309. LIVINGSTON, ARTHUR. "Italo-American fascism," *Survey,* v. 57 (March 1, 1927), pp. 738-740, 750.

1310. LUIGGI, LUIGI. "Per la cittadinanza degli italiani all' estero specialmente in America," *Nuova Antologia,* v. 231 (September 16, 1923), pp. 187-191.

1311. *Lynching of Italian subjects at Tallulah, La.* July 20, 1899. 56th Congress, 2nd session (1901). Senate Documents, no. 125.

1312. *Lynching of certain Italian subjects in Tallulah, La.* 56th Congress, 2nd session (1901). No. 194, v. 14.

1313. MAIALE, HUGO V. *The Italian vote in Philadelphia between 1928 and 1946.* Unpublished doctoral thesis, University of Pennsylvania, 1950.

1314. MANN, ARTHUR. *LaGuardia Comes to Power, 1933.* Philadelphia: Lippincott, 1965.

1315. MANN, ARTHUR. *LaGuardia, A Fighter Against His Times, 1882-1933.* Chicago: University of Chicago Press, 1969.

1316. MARIO, JESSIE W. "Italy and the United States," *Nineteenth Century,* v. 29 (May 1891), pp. 701-718.

1317. MARR, ROBERT H. "The New Orleans Mafia case," *American Law Review,* v. 25 (1891), pp. 414-431.

1318. MARTINEZ, E. and E. SUCHMAN. "Letters from America and the 1948 Elections in Italy," *Public Opinion Quarterly,* (Spring 1950).

1319. MICOCCI, ANTONIO A. "Vito Marcantonio," *Romanica,* vol. I (March 1936).

1320. MONTGOMERY, ROBERT H. *Sacco-Vanzetti--The Murder and the Myth.* New York: Devin, 1960.

1321. "Mussolini's hands across the seas," *Literary Digest,* v. 87 (December 26, 1925), p. 10.

1322. "Mussolini's orders to Italians here," *Literary Digest,* v. 96 (February 25, 1928), p. 12.

1323. ["Does] Mussolini rule millions here?" *Literary Digest,* v. 103 (November 16, 1929), p. 14.

1324. "Mussolini and the Casa Italiana," *The Nation,* v. 141 (November 27, 1935), p. 610.

1325. MYERS, JEROME K. "Assimilation in the political community," *Sociology and Social Research,* v. 35 (January-February 1951), pp. 175-182.

1326. NOCITO, PIETRO. *La legge di Lynch e il conflitto italo americano.* Roma: Tipografia della Camera dei Deputati, 1891.

1327. NORMAN, JOHN. "Pro-fascist activities in western Pennsylvania during the Ethiopian war," *Western Pennsylvania Historical Magazine,* v. 25 (1942), pp. 143-148.

1328. NORMAN, JOHN. "Repudiation of fascism by the Italian-American press," *Journalism Quarterly,* v. 21 (March 1944), pp. 1-6.

1329. O'BRIEN, JOHN C. "John O. Pastore, Senator from Rhode Island," *Sign,* vol. 34 (July 1955), pp. 13-15 [The first Italian-American to become a governor and a United States Senator.]

1330. "Out of Italy," *New Yorker,* vol. 26 (November 4, 1950), p. 38 (On Impellitteri, Pecora and Corsi in 1950 New York mayoralty election).

1331. PANTELEONE, MICHAEL. *The Mafia and Politics.* New York: Coward, 1966.

1332. PANUNZIO, CONSTANTINE. "Italian Americans, fascism and the war," *Yale Review,* v. 31 (June 1942), pp. 771-782.

1333. [Pecora, Ferdinand] "Portrait," *Time,* vol. 28 (November 30, 1936), p. 37.

1334. [Pecora, Ferdinand] "Portrait," *Newsweek,* vol. 12 (August 29, 1938), p. 89.

1335. PIERANTONI, AUGUSTO. *I fatti di Nuova Orleans e il diritto internazionale.* Roma: Fratelli Palotta, 1891.

1336. POLETTI, CHARLES. *Alien Registration and the Italians,* n.p. [1940 pamphlet].

1337. POLETTI, CHARLES. "Bread, Spaghetti, but no Fascisti," *New York Times Magazine,* (July 16, 1944), p. 8+.

1338. PARENTI, MICHAEL J. *Ethnic and Political Attitudes--A Depth Study of Italian Americans.* Unpublished doctoral thesis. Yale University, 1962.

1339. "Recruits for Balilla," *Time,* v. 32 (September 5, 1938), pp. 42-43. (The Balilla was a Fascist youth organization.)

1340. REEVES, RICHARD. "The Other Half of the State Government," The *New York Times Magazine* (April 1967), pp. 254 ff. [Anthony J. Travia, Speaker of New York Assembly].

1341. Response to resolution, correspondence regarding lynching in Louisiana of Italian subjects. May 25, 1897. *55th Congress, 1st session. Senate Documents* No. 104, v. 5.

1342. ROSSI, ERNEST E. *The United States and the 1948 Italian Election.* Unpublished doctoral thesis, University of Pittsburgh, 1964.

1343. ROUCEK, JOSEPH S. "Italo-Americans and World War II," *Sociology and Social Research,* v. 29 (July - August, 1945), pp. 465-471.

1344. RUSSELL, FRANCIS. *Tragedy in Dedham.* New York: McGraw Hill, 1962. [Sacco-Vanzetti case]

1345. [Sacco-Vanzetti Case] *Transcript of the Record of the trial of Nicòla Sacco and Bartolomeo Vanzetti in the Courts of Massachusetts.* New York: Henry Holt, 1928-1929.

1346. SALVEMINI, GAETANO. *Italian fascist activities in the U.S.* Washington, D.C.: American Council on Public Affairs, 1940.

1347. SALVEMINI, GAETANO. "Italian war prisoners," *New Republic,* v. 110 (January 10, 1944), pp. 48-50.

1348. SCHAFFER, ALAN. *Vito Marcantonio, Radical in Congress,* (Syracuse: Syracuse University Press, 1966). [Originally, Ph.D. dissertation, University of Virginia, 1962]

1349. SCHNAPPER, M.B. "Mussolini's American agents," *Nation,* v. 147 (October 15, 1938), pp. 374-376.

1350. SERINO, GUSTAVE R. *Italians in the Political Life of Boston: A study of the Role of the immigrant and ethnic group in the political life of an urban community.* Unpublished doctoral thesis, Harvard University, 1950.

1351. SFORZA, CARLO and GAETANO SALVEMINI. "Biddle's order: two views on the removal of the enemy alien stigma from Italians," *Nation,* v. 155 (November 7, 1942), pp. 476-478.

1352. SPERANZA, GINO "A Mission of peace," *Outlook,* September 1904.

1353. SPERANZA, GINO C. "Political representation of Italo-American colonies in the Italian parliament," *Charities,* v. 15 (1906), pp. 521-522.

1354. "Status of naturalized American citizens of Italian origin and of their children," *Current History,* v. 31 (December 1929), pp. 599-600.

1355. TORTORA, VINCENT R. "Italian Americans; their swing to G.O.P. ...," *Nation,* v. 177 (October 24, 1953), pp. 330-332.

1356. *Trattamento dei cittadini italiani nella confederazione nord-americana e il trattato 25 Novembre 1913 tra l'Italia e gli Stati Uniti.* Pesaro: Stabilimento Tipografico Popolare, 1915 [by Bernardo Attolico?]

1357. TUCKER, RAY T. "Tools of Mussolini in America," *New Republic,* v. 52 (September 14, 1927), pp. 89-91.

1358. ULLMAN, VICTOR. "Oh How You'll Hate Him," *Saturday Evening Post,* vol. 233 (March 17, 1951), p. 30+. [On Michael V. DiSalle.]

1359. VALENTE, JOHN. "The need of a naturalization treaty with Italy," *Forum,* v. 52 (December, 1914), pp. 810-814.

1360. VAN ETTEN, IDA. "Vetgogne italiane in America," *Critica Sociale* (January 1893).

1361. WOLFE, BURTON. "Frisco's Go-Go Mayor," *Sign,* vol. 48 (November 1968), pp. 18-21. [Joseph L. Alioto]

1362. ZINN, HOWARD. *Fiorello LaGuardia in Congress.* Unpublished doctoral thesis, Columbia University, 1958.

C. *Agriculture [Rural Settlement]*

1363. BENNET, ALICE. "Italians as farmers and fruit-growers," *Outlook,* v. 90, no. 2 (September 12, 1908), pp. 87-88.

1364. BENNET, ALICE. "The Italian as a farmer," *Charities,* v. 21 (October 3, 1908), pp. 57-60.

1365. BENNET, ALICE. "Italian-American farmers," *Survey*, v. 22 (May 1, 1909), pp. 172-175.

1366. BOVE, GIACOMO. *Alcune idee sulla nostra emigrazione e progetto di una colonia agricola nel territorio delle Missioni.* Genova: 1885.

1367. CANCE, ALEXANDER E. "Immigrant rural communities," *Survey*, v. 25 (1911), pp. 587-595.

1368. CANCE, ALEXANDER. "Italians in agriculture," [Part II of Recent Immigrants in Agriculture.] *Reports of the Immigration Commission. 61st Congress, 2nd session. Senate Documents* No. 633, v. 2, pp. 38-440. 1911. [See No. 100]

1369. CLAGHORN, KATE H. "Agricultural distribution of immigrants," *Report of the Industrial Commission*, v. 15 (1915), pp. 499-507.

1370. DEVECCHI, PAOLO. "L'emigrazione italiana per la California dovrebbe essere principalmente agricola," *L'Italia coloniale*, v. 2 (July, 1901), pp. 50-52.

1371. FAVA, SAVERIO [Baron]. "Le colonie agricole italiane nell' America del Nord," *Nuova Antologia*, v. 197, (16 Ottobre 1904).

1372. GABRICI, LEO. "Gli italiani nell' agricoltura degli Stati Uniți," *Rivista Coloniale*, (Ottobre-Novembre 1917).

1373. GINGER, MINA C. "In Berry field and bog. The seasonal migration of Italian pickers to New Jersey: its profits, its cost, illiteracy and disease," *Charities*, v. 15 (November 4, 1905), pp. 162-169.

1374. *L'Italia* (Chicago, May 21, 1904). [Failure of agricultural colony at New Palermo, Alabama]. See No. 269.

1375. "Italian cooperatives in Jersey," *Cooperation*, v. 15 (November 1929), pp. 210-211.

1376. "Italians in cotton-growing," *Manufacturers' Record*, v. 45 (April 7, 1904), p. 249.

1377. MATTHEWS, JOHN L. "Tontitown: a story of the conservation of men," *Everybody's Magazine*, v. 20 (January 1909), pp. 3-13.

1378. MEADE, EMILY F. "The Italian immigrant on the land," *Charities*, v. 13 (March 4, 1904), pp. 541-544.

1379. MEADE, EMILY F. "Italians on the land," *U.S. Labor Bureau. Bulletin.* No. 14 (May 1907), pp. 473-533. [Hammonton settlement]

1380. MOORE, ANITA. "A Safe way to get on the soil: the work of Father Bandini at Tontitown," *World's Work*, v. 24 (June 1912), pp. 215-219.

1381. NICHOLS, FLOYD B. "Making an immigrant's paradise," *Technical World*, v. 19 (August 1913), pp. 894-897.

1382. PALMER, HANS C. *Italian Immigration and the Development of California Agriculture*. Unpublished doctoral thesis, University of California [Berkeley], 1965.

1383. PECORINI, ALBERTO. "The Italian as an agricultural laborer," *Annals, American Academy of Political and Social Science*. v. 33 (1909), pp. 380-390.

1384. POPONOE, WILSON. "Dr. Fenzi's contributions to American horticulture. The work of a pioneer plantsman in California," *Journal of Heredity*, v. 13 (May 1922), pp. 215-220.

1385. PREZIOSI, GIOVANNI. "L'emigrazione italiana nel Nord-America e la colonizzazione agricola," *Rassegna Contemporanea*, v. 111 (January 1910), pp. 111-118.

1386. QUAIROLI, C. "La Colonia italiana di Vineland (New Jersey)," *Bollettino dell' Emigrazione* (1908).

1387. RAVAIOLI, ANTONIO. "Colonizzione agraria degli Stati Uniti in rapporto all' emigrazione italiana," *Bollettino dell' Emigrazione* (1904).

1388. *Relazione esectiva per una Società italiana di colonizzazione agricola al Texas*. Milano: Tip. La Stampa Commerciale, 1909.

1389. ROSELLI, BRUNO. "Arkansas epic," *Century*, v. 99 (January 1920), pp. 377-386.

1390. [Rossi, Adolfo.] "Italian Farmers in the South," [An interview with Adolfo Rossi by Gino C. Speranza]. *Charities*, v. 15 (1905), pp. 307-308.

1391. SCOTT, CHARLES. "Italian farmers for Southern agriculture," *Manufacturers' Record*, v. 48 (November 9, 1905), pp. 423-424.

1392. STONE, ALFRED H. "The Italian cotton grower: the Negro's problem," *South Atlantic Quarterly*, v. 4 (January 1905), pp. 42-47.

1393. STONE, ALFRED H. "Italian cotton-growers in Arkansas," *Review of Reviews*, v. 35 (February 1907), pp. 209-213.

1394. TABET, TITO. "Colonizzazione agraria nel Texas," *Agricoltura Coloniale* (Gennaio-Febbraio 1908).

1395. "Tontitown in Arkansas," *The Interpreter,* v. 8 (April 1929), pp. 56-58.

1396. "Tontitown: an Italian farming community," *Service Bureau for Intercultural Education* [New York], Publications (1937).

1397. TOSTI, GUSTAVO. "The agricultural possibilities of Italian immigration," *Charities,* v. 12 (May 7, 1904), pp. 472-476.

VI. ITALIAN AMERICAN LIFE: BELLES-LETTRES AND
    THE ARTS
        A. *General Studies*
        B. *Preliminary Checklist of Novels Written*
           in English Dealing with the Italian
           American Experience

VI.   ITALIAN AMERICAN LIFE: BELLES-LETTRES AND THE ARTS.

It is, perhaps, not invidious to note that although Italians have been energetically engaged in the arts in American society, the evidences of their presence in the literature of the arts is not, itself, fully recorded. There are no journals clearly identified with Italians; and no literary *genre* exists clearly Italian in its form. In the graphic arts, no distinctly Italian forms have emerged, yet it would be hazardous to deny the Italian presence. The difficulty may lie in differentiating the pervasive influence of peninsular Italians from that of Italian Americans; certainly, a very real part of the American experience in the arts is that contributed by Italian Americans; and the evolving efforts by Italian Americans to delineate (whatever the art form) the experience of Italians in American society has a history which remains to be written.* The titles in this section are very general in scope: representative but equally indicative of the paucity of material in this area. The checklist of novels written in English dealing with the Italian American experience is a somewhat amended list compiled by Professor Rudolph J. Vecoli for a symposium on the Italian American novel sponsored by the American Italian Historical Association in New York City (October 25, 1969), an event somewhat unusual in American intellectual circles, yet, perhaps, prophetic.

A.   *General Studies*

1398.   ALDA, FRANCES.   *Men, women and tenors.* Boston: Houghton-Mifflin, 1937 [Italian contribution to opera in America].

1399.   CAUTELA, GIUSEPPE.   "The Italian theatre in New York," *American Mercury,* vol. 12 (September 1927), pp. 106-112.

---

*"Since we are gathered not to celebrate but to examine the state of Italian-American literature, I trust that it will not be thought ungracious of me to address myself to the following question: why has the Italian-American contribution to American literature been so small--or as Puzo put it: Why have writers of Italian descent made hardly any impact on the American public? Certainly the American reading public has not been unreceptive to ethnic authors. What would be left of American literature without Jewish writers like Bernard Malamud and Philip Roth, black writers like Ralph Ellison and James Baldwin, Irish writers like James T. Farrell and Edwin O'Connor? The reasons for the paucity of Italian names in the role of American writers are to be sought, I submit, in the history and sociology of the Italian-American ethnic group." Rudolph J. Vecoli, "The Italian American literary subculture: an historical and sociological analysis," John M. Cammett, ed., *The Italian American Novel* [No. 1401], pp. 6-7.

1400. CUNETTO, DOMINIC J.   *Italian language theatre clubs in St. Louis, Missouri, 1910-1950*. Gainesville: University of Florida, 1960.

1401. CAMMETT, JOHN M., ed.   *The Italian American Novel*. New York: American Italian Historical Association, 1969. [Proceedings of a symposium]. Discussion and commentary by J. Caruso, R. Corsel, R. B. Green, J. Mangione, V. McLaughlin, L. Moss, F. Rosengarten, R. J. Vecoli, and J. Vergara.

1402. GATTI-CASAZZA, GIULIO.   "Memories of opera," *Saturday Evening Post*, v. 206 (October 28, November 11, November 25, December 9, December 23, 1933.)

1403. GIANTURCO, ELIO.   "Italian music and musicians in America," *Bulletin and Italiana*. Italy-America Society, vol. 2 (January, 1928), pp. 3-6.

1404. HAPGOOD, HUTCHINS.   "The foreign stage in New York: *The Italian theatre,"* Bookman, v. 11 (1900), pp. 545-553.

1405. HESS, C.D.   "Early opera in America," *Cosmopolitan*, v. 32 (December 1901), 139-152.

1406. IRWIN, ELIZABETH.   "Where the players are marionettes: the age of chivalry is born again in a little Italian theatre in Mulberry Street," *Craftsman*, v. 12 (1907), pp. 667-669.

1407. "Italian theatres in Brooklyn," *Current Literature*, v. 27 (1900), pp. 3-4.

1408. KIMBALL, CHARLOTTE.   "An outline of amusements among Italians in New York," *Charities*, v. 5 (August 18, 1900), pp. 1-8.

1409. GREEN, ROSE B.   *The Evolution of Italian-American Fiction as a Document of the interaction of two cultures*. Unpublished doctoral thesis, University of Pennsylvania, 1962. [major work] See No. 1411.

1410. MURRAY, WILLIAM B.   "Italian musicians in America," *Bulletin and Italiana*. Italy-America Society, v. 1 (March 1927), pp. 21-23.

1411. PERAGALLO, OLGA.   *Italian-American authors and their contribution to American literature*. New York: S. F. Vanni, 1949. See No. 1409.

1412. PETERSON, ROY M.   "Echoes of the Italian Risorgimento in contemporaneous American writers," *Modern Language Association of America, Publications*, vol. 47 (March 1932), pp. 220-240.

1413. [Petrillo, James Caesar] "Portrait," *American Federationist,* vol. 55 (December, 1948), p. 19.

1414. SHAW, ARNOLD. *Sinatra-Twentieth Century Romantic.* New York: Cowles, 1968.

1415. [Vaudeville] "Enter the Italian on the Vaudeville Stage," *The Survey,* vol. 24 (May 7, 1910), p. 199.

1416. VIRGILIO, RUDOLPH. "The development of Italian opera in New York," *Italian Library of Information,* New York. [Outline Studies] No. 6 (September 1938).

B.   *Preliminary Checklist of Novels Written in English Dealing with the Italian American Experience*

1417. ANGELO, V.   *Bells of Bleeker Street*. New York, 1949.

1418. BENASUTTI, MARION.   *No Steady Job For Papa*. New York, 1966.

1419. BIAGI, ERNEST L.   *Luigi Bazzeca*. New York, 1931.

1420. CAUTELA, GIUSEPPE.   *Moon Harvest*. New York, 1925.

1421. CORSEL, RALPH.   *Up There the Stars*. New York, 1968.

1422. D'AGOSTINO, GUIDO.   *Hills Beyond Manhattan*. New York, 1942.

1423. D'AGOSTINO, GUIDO.   *My Enemy, The World*. New York, 1947.

1424. D'AGOSTINO, GUIDO.   *Olives on the Apple Tree*. New York, 1940.

1425. D'ANGELO, PASQUALE.   *Sons of Italy*. New York, 1924.

1426. DE CAPITE, MICHAEL.   *Maria*. New York, 1943.

1427. DE CAPITE, MICHAEL.   *The Bennet Place*. New York, 1948.

1428. DE CAPITE, MICHAEL.   *No Bright Banner*. New York, 1944.

1429. DE CAPITE, RAYMOND.   *The Coming of Fabrizze*. New York, 1960.

1430. DI DONATO, PIETRO.   *Christ in Concrete*. New York, 1939.

1431. DI DONATO, PIETRO.   *Three Circles of Light*. New York, 1960.

1432. FALBO, ITALO CARLO.   *Good Bye New York*. New York [n.d.].

1433. FANTE, JOHN THOMAS.   *Ask the Dust*. New York, 1939.

1434. FANTE, JOHN THOMAS.   *Dago Red*. New York, 1940.

1435. FANTE, JOHN THOMAS.   *Full of Life*. Boston, 1952.

1436. FANTE, JOHN THOMAS.   *Wait Until Spring, Bandini*. New York, 1938.

1437. FUMENTO, ROCCO.   *Tree of Dark Reflection*. New York, 1962.

1438. FUMENTO, ROCCO.   *Devil by the Tail*. New York, 1954.

126

1439. FORGIONE, LOUIS.   *Reamer Lou.* New York, 1924.

1440. FORGIONE, LOUIS.   *The River Between.* New York, 1928.

1441. LAPOLLA, GARIBALDI MARTO.   *Fire in the Flesh.* New York, 1931.

1442. LAPOLLA, GARIBALDI MARTO.   *The Grand Gennaro.* New York, 1935.

1443. LAPOLLA, GARIBALDI MARTO.   *Miss Rollins in Love.* New York, 1932.

1444. LONGO, LUCAS.   *The Family on Vendetta Street.* New York, 1968.

1445. MANGIONE, JERRE.   *Mount Allegro.* Boston, 1942.

1446. MARZANI, CARL.   *The Survivor.* New York, 1958.

1447. MELLER, SIDNEY.   *Home is Here.* New York, 1941.

1448. MOROSO, JOHN ANTONIO.   *Stumbling Hard.* New York, 1923.

1449. PAGANO, JO.   *Golden Wedding.* New York, 1943.

1450. PAGANO, JO.   *The Paesanos.* Boston, 1940.

1451. PANETTA, GEORGE.   *Jimmy Potts Gets a Haircut.* New York, 1947.

1452. PANETTA, GEORGE.   *We Ride a White Donkey.* New York, 1944.

1453. PETRACCA, JOSEPH.   *Come Back to Sorrento.* Boston, 1948.

1454. POWELL, FELIX.   *The Transformation of Felix.* Portland Maine, 1915.

1455. PUZO, MARIO.   *The Fortunate Pilgrim.* New York, 1965.

1456. PUZO, MARIO.   *The Godfather.* New York, 1969.

1457. TOMASI, MARI.   *Deep Grow the Roots.* Philadelphia, 1940.

1458. TOMASI, MARI.   *Like Lesser Gods.* Milwaukee, 1949.

1459. VALENTI, ANGELO.   *Hill of Little Miracles.* New York, 1942.

1460. VALENTI, ANGELO.   *Look Out Yonder.* New York, 1943.

1461. VILLA, SILVIO.   *The Unbidden Guest.* New York, 1923.

1462. VERGARA, JOE.   *Love and Pasta.* New York, 1969.

INDEX OF NAMES

[References Are To Entry Numbers]

Cianfarra, C. 443, 757
Ciarlantini, F. 444
Cimilluca, S. 758
Cinfoletti, M. 964
Ciolli, D.T. 1218
Cipriani, L. 649, 650
Cipriani, L. [Count] 455
Ciraolo, G. 1158
Claghorn, K.H. 1159, 1369, 1217
Clark, E. 1269
Clark, E.T. 615
Clark, F.E. 402
Clot, A. 53
Cocchia, E. 147
Cohen, S. 1007
Colajanni, N. 445, 904, 1160,
      1161, 1162
Colbacchini, P. 1063
Coletti, F. 148
Colletti, U.M. 149, 319
Cometti, E. 320
Compagnoni-Merefoschi, M. 616
Concestré, M. 972
Confalonieri, F. 857
Conoscenti, E. 321
Consolino, F. 154
Conte, A. 535
Conte. G. 446, 1068
Contento, A. 155
Cooke, H.T. 536
Corbino, E. 157
Cordasco, F. 92, 447, 538, 539,
      768, 862, 903, 949,
      963, 965, 966, 971,
      1000, 1008, 1100
Cordova, A. 158
Corinaldi, L. 86
Cornwell, E.E. 539
Corradini, E. 322, 323
Corresca, R. 764
Corrias, 327
Corridore, F. 159
Corsel, R. 1401, 1421
Corsi, E. 325, 326, 540,
      765, 767, 1330
Corte, P. 617
Cosenza, M.E. 967
Costello, F. 1191, 1193
Cotillo, S.A. 457

Coulter, C.W. 651
Covello, L. 447, 482, 768, 769,
      770, 901, 968, 969,
      970, 971
Coxe, J.E. 1163, 1273
Crawford, J.S. 1219
Crespi, C. 696
Criscuolo, L. 48, 328, 1274,
      1275, 1276, 1277
Crocetti, M.C. 771
Cuneo, G. 697
Cunetto, D.J. 1400
Cunningham, G.E. 618
Cupelli, A. 1278
Curinga, N. 772
Curti, G. 160
Cushing, R.J. 1069
Cusumano, G. 541
Cutino, S. 48

D'Agostino, G. 1422, 1423, 1424
D'Agostino, P. 774, 1244
D'Alesandre, J.J. 901, 1220
Dall'Aste-Brandolini, A. 542
Dalla Volta, R. 161, 162, 163, 329
D'Amato, G. 1164
D'Ambrosio, M. 87
Dana, J. 1221
D'Angelo, P. 1425
Davenport, W.E. 330, 331, 543, 775
David-Dubois, R. 773, 901
Davin, C. 165
DeAmicis, E. 449
DeBiasi, A. 166
DeBiasi, M. 544, 778
DeBonis-DeNobili, I. 167
DeCapite, M. 776, 1426, 1427, 1428
DeCapite, R. 1429
Defina, G. 1292
DeGregorio, U.F. 168
DeKoster, P. 450
DeLeone, E. 169
Deliti-D'Oblio 451
DellaTorre, R. 170
DellaValle-DiMiabello, A. 171
DeLuca, F. 172
deLuca, G. 1070
DeLucis, A. 332
DelVecchio, G.S. 175

Galli, G. 195
Gans, H.J. 196, 909
Gardini, G. 974
Garlick, R. 463, 789
Garoschi, A. 337
Gaster, D.F. 1170
Gatti, A. 790
Gatti-Casazza, G. 1402
Gebhart, J.C. 1015
Geddes, J. 791
Genovese, V. 1169
Gertrude, A. 549
Ghio, P. 1291
Ghiradella, R. 1227
Giacosa, G. 464, 550, 654
Giannini, A.P. 1221, 1237
Giannotta, R.O. 403
Gianturco, E. 1403
Gilkey, G.R. 197
Gillett, L.H. 1016
Ginger, M.C. 1373
Gini, C. 198, 199
Giorgio, R. 338
Giovinco, J. 1228
Gisolfi, A.M. 975
Glanz, R. 792
Glazer, N. 910
Gley, W. 200
Godio, G. 201
Goggio, E. 794
Golden, H.H. 976
Gould, F.A. 3
Grabo, C.H. 339
Grandi, A. 340
Grandgent, C.H. 977
Greco, V. 1229
Greeley, A.M. 1079
Green, R.B. 1401, 1409
Greene, A.B. 3
Gregori, V. 1080, 1081
Grieco, R. 911, 912
Griel, C.L. 1018
Griffin, A.P.C. 4
Griffith, E. 1017
Grose, H.B. 341, 795
Grossi, V. 202, 203, 465,
    466, 796
Grossman, R.P. 404
Guglielmi, F. 1082

Gurney, M.E. 913

Hackett, J.K. 1083
Hale, E.E. 1230
Hall, P.F. 204, 279
Hanighen, F.C. 1294
Hapgood, H. 1404
Harris, E.L. 343
Hartt, R.L. 1231
Haughwont, F.G. 205
Heilbroner, R. 1297
Hess, C.D. 1405
Hewes, L. 622
Hillenbrand, M.J. 1084
Hilliard, M.H. 551
Hoffman, G. 1085
Howe, M. 552
Howells, W.D. 553, 914
Howerth, I.A. 1171
Huntington, H.G. 206, 207
Hutchinson, E.P. 978

Iachini, C. 1086
Iamurri, G.A. 468
Ianni, F.A. 916, 917, 918, 1172
Impellitteri, V. 1330
Invernizio, C. 345
Iorizzo, L.J. 405, 1234, 1235
Irwin, E.A. 1236, 1406
Irwin, G. 554

Jadot, L. 219
Jenkins, H. 809
Jenks, J.W. 218
Jones, H.D. 1088
Jones, I. 705
Jones, M.J. 810
Josephson, M. 1237

Kapp, F. 558
Karlin, A.J. 1298, 1299, 1300, 1301
Keller, F.A. 352
Kelly, M. 811, 812, 1089
Kendall, J.S. 1302
Kimball, C. 1408
Kingsley, H.L. 919
Knepler, A.E. 559
Kolden, T.S. 995
Koren, J. 1238

La Guardia, F. 1314, 1315, 1362
La Gumina, S.J. 1305, 1306, 1307, 1308
La Macchia, L.N. 602
La Piana, A. 406
La Piana, G. 660
Lagnese, J.G. 1090
Landesco, J. 1175
Landolfi, A. 470
Landar, A. 220
Langley, L.J. 625, 626
Lapolla, G.M. 1441, 1442, 1443
Lathrop, M.D. 813, 1239
Lauck, J.W. 218
Le Berthon, T. 1093, 1094
Le Conte, R. 815
Leatrice, D. 925, 926
Leavitt, M. 661
Leland, W.G. 1240
Lerda, G. 816
Levasseur, E. 226
Lewis, C.A. 920
Liberi, I. 227
Lipari, M. 1241
Livi-Bacci, M 96
Livingston, A. 1309
Livolsi, G. 353
Lo Bello, N. 921
Lo Grasso, A.H. 471
Lolli, G. 922
Lomonaco, A. 228
Longo, L. 1444
Lopreato, J. 354, 407, 923, 924
Lord, E. 408
Lubell, S. 562
Lucattini, A.L. 229
Luciano, L. 1193
Luiggi, L. 1310
Lussana, F. 472
Lynch, B.J. 563
Lynch, D. 1095

McCarty, J 571
McClelland, W. 828
McKelvey, B. 572
McLaughlin, A.J. 356
Mclaughlin, V. 1401
McMain, E. 1020
McNulty, J. 829
McLeod, C. 1097
Macbrayne, L.E. 355

Macchiaro, G. 820
Mac Donald, J.S. 925, 926
Mackey, U.L. 1096
Maffei, G. 473
Maiale, H.V. 1313
Mainiero, J. 564
Maisel, A. 818, 819
Malnate, N. 230, 409
Manfredini, D.M. 662
Mangano, A. 357, 358, 565, 821,
         1098, 1099, 1100
Mangione, J. 1401, 1445
Mann, A. 1314, 1315
Manson, G.J. 566
Mantegazza, V. 231
Marcantonio, V. 1305, 1307, 1319, 1348
Marcuson, L.R. 927
Mariano, G. 1101
Mariano, J.H. 232, 410, 1176
Marinacci, B. 827
Marini, B. 823
Marinoni, A. 822
Mario, J.W. 1316
Marr, R.H. 1177, 1317
Marraro, H.R. 474, 475, 476, 567,
         568, 569, 570, 824,
         825, 826, 979,
         980, 981, 982
Martinez, E. 1318
Marzani, C. 1446
Marzo, R. 65
Mastrogiovanni, S. 1242
Mastro-Valerio, A. 663
Matthews, J.L. 1377
Matthews, M.F. 983
May, E. 984
Mayor, Des. P.E. 233
         [see Des Planches, E.M.]
Mazzei, P. 463, 476, 826
Mead, M. 985
Meade, E.F. 627, 1378, 1379
Meller, S. 1447
Merlion, S. 359
Micheli, G. 708
Micocci, A.A. 1319
Migliore, S. 573
Milesi, F. 1102
Miller, H.A. 839
Moffat, A. 574
Mollica, P. 66

Monacada, F.   830
Mondello, S.   405, 411, 831, 1104
Montalbo, O.   1243
Montgomery, R.H.   1320
Monticelli, G.L.   96, 240
Moore, A.   1380
Moorhead, E.   987
Moreno, C.C.   360
Morgan, A.   1179
Moroni, G.   235, 629, 630, 631
Moroso, J.A.   1448
Morvillo, G.   236, 237
Mosca, G.   1178
Moseley, D.H.   1021
Moss, L.   1401
Moynihan, D.P.   910
Mudge, G.G.   1022
Muholland, T.   361
Murphy, M.   1244
Murphy, M.C.   1105
Murray, W.B.   1410
Musmanno, M.A.   412
Mussolini, B.   1286, 1321, 1322, 1323,
        1324, 1349, 1357
Myers, J.K.   1325

Napolitano, G.   97
Naselli, G.   576
Neidle, C.S.   478
Nelli, H.S.   664, 832, 928,
        1181, 1245
Nichols, F.B.   1381
Nicolà, G.B.   241
Nicoletti, A.   66
Nicotri, G.   477
Nizzardini, G.   1023, 1024, 1025
Noa, T.L.   1106
Norman, J.   1327, 1328
Norton, G.P.   665

Odencrantz, L.   833, 1246
Oldrini, A.   247
O'Brien, J.C.   1329
Oppenheimer, F.   1182
Orsini, R.M.   835
Ottolenghi, C.   250

Pagano, J.   838, 1449, 1450
Pagnini, P.   364
Palisi, B.J.   929, 930, 931

Palma di Castiglione, G.   252
        [see Castiglione, G.E. Di P.]
Palmer, H.C.   1382
Palmieri, A.   1107, 1108, 1109
Pancrazi, A.   253
Panetta, G.   1451, 1452
Panteleone, M.   1331
Panunzio, C.M.   479, 480, 481, 1332
Papa, D.F.   580
Papini, C.   632
Parenti, M.J.   1338
Parini, P.   365
Parisi, L.   366
Park, R.E.   839
Pastore, J.O.   1329
Patri, A.   957, 988
Patrizi, E.   710
Pecora, F.   1330, 1333, 1334
Pecorini, A.   840, 841, 1383
Pedrazzi, O.   254
Peebles, R.   482
Peixotto, E.   711
Pellegrini, A.M.   483, 484
Peloso, R.   1110
Penattoni, G.V.   709
Peragallo, O.   1411
Perilli, G.   712
Perotti, A.   367
Perry, G.S.   581
Pertusio, M.   256
Pesaturo, U.U.M.   582, 583
Peterson, R.M.   1412
Petracca, J.   1453
Petrillo, J.C.   1413
Petrosino, J.   1165, 1184, 1190, 1200
Phenis, A.   633
Phipard, C.B.   1249
Piccinni, G.   1111
Pierantoni, A.   1183, 1335
Pileggi, N.   584, 842, 843
Pincitore, A.   257
Pisani, L.F.   413
Pisani, P.   98
Pistella, D.   1112
Pitts, G.L.   666
Pius, P.P. X.   113, 1114
Pius, P.P. XI.   1115
Pius, P.P. XII.   1116, 1117
Poletti, C.   1336, 1337
Pomeroy, S.G.   932

Pope, F. 486
Pope, G. 485
Poponoe, W. 1384
Powderly, T.V. 259
Powell, F. 1454
Preziosi, G. 260, 261, 262, 263,
        264, 368, 414, 1385
Prezzolino, G. 487, 488, 844, 989
Price, W. 369
Prindiville, K.G. 667
Provano Del Sabbione, L. 668
Psathas, G. 933
Pucelli, R. 489
Puzo, M. 845, 946, 1455, 1456
Puzzo, V.P. 669
Pyrke, B.A. 586

Quaintance, E.C. 670
Quairoli, C. 1386

Racca, V. 266
Radin, E.D. 1184
Radin, P. 713
Raffo, G.B. 267
Rallo, J.A. 500
Rambaud, J. 268
Ramirez, M.D. 638
Rankin, L. 671
Ratto, M.O. 490
Ravaioli, A. 1387
Reed, D. 1026
Reeves, R. 1340
Reid, S. 1185
Reynolds, M.J. 1120
Ridolfi, L. 491
Ricci, V.R. 846
Riccio, P.M. 901
Riggio, V. 1257
Riis, J.A. 538, 588, 589
Rizzati, F. 415
Robbins, J.E. 848
Roberts, K.L. 847
Roberts, M. 1027
Robinson, G.K. 1028, 1121
Rolle, A.F. 416, 714, 715, 716
Rosati, T. 1029
Rose, A.M. 1030
Rose, P.M. 417
Roseboro, V. 590

Roselli, B. 371, 492, 640, 641,
        849, 850, 851, 935,
        990, 991, 1389
Rosengarten, F. 1401
Rossati, G. 418, 591, 639
Rosetti-Agresti, O. 1250
Rossi, A. 374, 493, 494, 495,
        496, 853, 1390
Rossi, A. 1251
Rossi, A.S. 992
Rossi, E. 270, 271, 272,
        372, 373, 1252
Rossi, E.E. 1342
Rossi, J. 497
Rossi, P.A. 1123
Rossi, P.H. 992
Ross, E.A. 370, 854
Rosso, A. 853
Rott, W.T. 974
Roucek, J. 742, 769, 936, 1343
Rubieri, E. 717
Ruben, V.D. 855
Ruddy, A.C. 1097
Ruggiero, A. 419, 498
Ruotolo, O. 856
Rushmore, E.M. 15
Russell, F. 1344
Russo, G. 375
Russo, N. 1124

Sacco, N. 1344, 1345
Sada, L. 635
Sager, G.A. 672
Saint Martin, G. 636
Salvemini, G. 1346, 1347, 1351
SanGiuliano, A. di. 180, 273,
        [See Di San Giuliano, A.]
Sanminiatelli, D. 376
Santini, F. 499
Santini, L. 274
Santoro, D. 500
Sartorio, H.C. 1125, 1126
Sartoris, A. 592
Sassone, T. 1186
Sayre, J. 1267
Scala, L. 637
Scalabrini, G.B. 99, 275, 276, 277,
        1055, 1074, 1081
Scalia, E.S. 857

WITHDRAWAL